Meaningful Conversations for Dating Couples

Bentley and Susan Hill

To our families,
who have modeled God-honoring relationships, and
to our students
at the University of Hawaii, OSU-Okmulgee, and Carl Albert
State College who have allowed us front row seats to watch
God work in your lives.

Contents

Introduction:

The Purpose of Dating

The information age is nothing short of glorious. Using a small, handheld device, we can organize a get-together, find the nearest eating establishments, receive updates on game scores, access social media, and even write complete research papers. Somehow we have become convinced that we can manage our relationships with the same ease. Ask young people, and they will tell you that their preferred method of communication is through text. Maybe this is because it is more convenient, or perhaps it is because texting allows us to "edit" our conversations before pressing send. Either way, conversing with our thumbs rather than our mouths has made it increasingly more difficult for any of us to carry on good heart-to-heart, face-to-face conversations. The abbreviated style of texting has carried over into our verbal exchanges, and the content of those conversations tends to evolve around the latest feeds on social media. Meaningful conversations have become challenging, even for the sincere dating couple seeking to honor God in their relationship.

That's exactly why this book has come into being. After working with college students and young adults for nearly three decades, we believe there are still couples who long for good old-fashioned conversations that lead to healthy relationships. Many of these couples have set high standards and long to honor God with their relationships. They have been taught and believe that being a follower of Christ means inviting Him into every relationship they are involved in. Time and again we have had couples approach us and ask if we could recommend a devotional that would help. We only realized the shortage of such material when our own daughter began dating a young man who was determined to keep God at the center of the budding romance. Together, we looked for material that would help them engage in meaningful conversations; much of what we found was for engaged couples, preparing to say "I do," and neither Samantha nor Nick was ready to declare their relationship altar-bound. They simply wanted a guide for keeping their focus on God while discovering His will for their relationship and lives.

That's precisely the goal of this book. It is a ten-week study designed to allow you to determine God's will for your life and your relationship by growing individually and by discovering one another through meaningful, Christ-centered conversations. The content of each chapter is designed to give couples the opportunity to explore and reflect on their own individual spiritual journeys and beliefs and then to discuss them with one another through intentional, yet comfortable dialogue.

We think it is also important that we clarify that the purpose of this study is not to make your relationship work. Playing cupid is pretty risky business. **The purpose of any dating relationship is two-fold: To glorify God and to discover His will in a specific relationship.** Many of us were brought up under the teaching that the goal of dating is marriage. While it is true we should never date anyone we wouldn't consider marrying, it is also true that the weeks and months of dating may reveal that this is not the person God intends for us to spend the rest of our lives with. If the goal of dating is marriage, then a break-up equals failure. That's why we strongly believe that the goal of dating is not to walk down an aisle but to glorify God.

Please understand that you may begin this study with one another and somewhere along the way decide that this is not God's plan or time. To discover this to be a "no" does not equal failure. After all, your goal is not to stay together; your goal is to discover your compatibility and God's will. A "no" or "not now" can accomplish that goal and, therefore, is actually a success rather than a defeat.

Your relationship will be much more productive if you will focus less on making the relationship work and focus instead on making it healthy. A mark of a healthy dating relationship is when at the end of the relationship, whether it be two months or seventy years, the individuals are able to say, "This relationship moved me closer to God." Imagine how honoring to God it would be for each individual you date to say of you, "I am closer to God today because of the time we spent together." Now that is a Facebook status that would gain attention.

So, let this book be a guide in helping you develop a healthy relationship through meaningful conversations. The chapters begin with the basics and move to more personal topics as your relationship and the study continue. In Chapter 1, you will reflect on your own salvation experience and then share with one another about this most important event. Chapter 2 discusses the importance of prayer and gives you the opportunity as a couple to talk about prayers you have seen answered and those that may seem unanswered. Chapter 3 invites a study about fears and initiates a meaningful conversation about silly and legitimate fears. Chapter 4 is instrumental in helping you set standards as a couple that will encourage God-honoring entertainment.

As you continue in your dating relationship, the study moves to more personal topics. Chapter 5 prompts you to identify your passion and how you may live it out through ministry, hobbies, and even a dream job. Chapter 6 invites you to consider your experiences with the church and the role it has played in your spiritual journey. Chapter 7 focuses on the role family has played and continues to play in your life while Chapter 8 shifts the study and discussion to the importance and influence of friends.

The last two studies assume that you are becoming better acquainted and are more comfortable sharing about personal issues. Chapter 9 introduces the challenge of staying healthy and allows the two of you to develop a plan for taking care of the temple of God, including the setting of physical boundaries. Finally, the last chapter will give you the opportunity to evaluate how the relationship is progressing, noting elements that seem healthy and those that may need more attention.

We thought it would be fun for you to hear from another couple who has been where you are and survived, so we invited our daughter and son-in-law to add a few comments from a younger generation's perspective. At the end of each chapter, you will find a short section called "Keeping it real with Nick and Samantha" in which the two of them have provided practical advice and ideas for planning dates and doing life in a way that honors God.

To get the most out of this book, be ready to do some homework. You will notice each chapter is written in such a way as to allow for independent Bible study on a given topic, followed by questions that will let you gather your thoughts about personal experiences. Some questions are preceded by a bold, italicized **Q&A**. These questions and your answers will become the springboard for conversations the two of you will have on the subject later. Be honest and willing to communicate; remember that we are moving away from the one-word answers to texts. The letter "k" is no longer allowed.

In addition to doing the study independently, agree to set aside time weekly to discuss what you have learned. Each chapter ends with a section called "Making the Most of your Meaningful Conversation." This is a list of the **Q&A**'s you dealt with in the chapter and will serve as a guide for your discussion together. We suggest that the guy take the initiative in setting up the Bible study times. It's never too early for him to practice being the spiritual leader God has called him to be. As you agree on when to get together, make sure that you allow adequate time to study and discuss together, which means you probably don't want to just tack ten minutes on to the end of a great date. Let the quality time spent in Bible study and dialogue be the main event; if there is time afterwards for a movie, go for it.

The conversations are ideally meant to occur face-to-face, maybe over a steaming cup of coffee or your favorite soft drink. If you find yourself in a long-distance relationship, the study can still work well, but you probably will want to Skype or call since the whole purpose is to have good "talks" rather than "texts."

As you begin this journey toward a Christ-centered relationship, our prayer is that you "may become blameless and harmless, children of God without fault in the midst of a crooked and perverse generation, among who you shine as lights in the world" (Philippians 2:15). We pray that the discussions that stem from this study will help you jump into spiritual topics and create a safer environment for your heart to know His will. We also pray that you will serve as an example to a world that often seeks relationships based on attraction rather than substance. You will be a testimony that positive relationships are more than feelings; they are the result of meaningful conversations.

"Meaningful conversations are the linchpin of any successful relationship. You may not have the control to lengthen your life, but you can do much to deepen it." Author and Small Business expert, Frank Sonnenberg

Chapter 1:

Spiritual Milestones

What is a hippocampus?
- a) a university with over 25,000 students
- b) a group of hippopotamuses
- c) a part of the brain
- d) a mythological creature that protected royalty

*M*aybe it would help to know that you use your hippo-campus every day and often blame it for getting you into trouble with forgotten birthdays and missed appointments. If you guessed that a hippocampus is part of the brain, you are absolutely right. (If you guessed that a hippocampus is a group of hippopotamuses, you are undoubtedly the life of every party you attend.)

The hippocampus is actually the part of the brain that is responsible for storing memories and making new ones. It is shaped like a seahorse, hence the name "hippo," which is Greek for horse, and "kampos," meaning sea. This little gem of human anatomy is squished in the folds of the temporal lobe; perhaps this explains why it is difficult for many of us to find and use. Numerous authors and websites have under-taken the challenge of helping us develop and strengthen our hippocampuses, offering workouts and exercises that may increase the size of the gray matter and our opportunities for success.

While there is scientific evidence that our hippocampus tends to shrink physically with age, could it also be true spiritually? Do we sometimes forget how real God is and how good He has been?

"I get so frustrated with myself for doubting God. It's like every time I face a challenge, I forget how He has brought me through all the challenges before, and I panic, wondering if He is real and if He'll come through," admits one twenty-three-year old. Most of us can relate to her honesty. We have an incredible encounter with God where we know without a doubt He is real, powerful, and personally involved in our lives. We lift our hands in praise and declare Him our Sovereign King and Almighty God. We declare our love for Him and make promises that wherever He leads we'll go. Then adversity comes: an overwhelming financial need, a health concern, the death of a loved one. For some of us, it can be something much less traumatic: a flat tire, a sleepless night, a non-working hair straightener. Suddenly, all memories of who God is and what He has done are gone. In that moment, our hippocampus malfunctions, and we suffer from a case of spiritual amnesia.

Q&A: *Can you think of a time recently when you suffered from spiritual amnesia, and you temporarily doubted if God was real or cared about you, or perhaps you were overwhelmed with worry for no good reason?*

God is keenly aware of our deteriorating hippocampus. He dealt with it in our ancestors long before we made it to planet Earth. In Psalm 78 we find a retelling of God's involvement with a rebellious Israel. Take a moment to read 78:9-11. According to verse 11, not only did the children of Ephraim refuse to walk in God's law, but they "_____ His works and His wonders that He had shown them" (NKJV). A few verses down in

Psalm 78:42, we are told that the children of Israel "did not _____ His power: The day when He redeemed them from the enemy." The children of Israel had experienced God in miraculous ways, but as they made their way through the desert, their hippocampus suffered from the heat, and their relationship with God suffered as a result.

Longing to have healthy relationships with His creation, God started a workout program to increase their memories. He would instruct them to build altars at certain locations where divine encounters occurred. These altars were often built by pushing up a mound of earth or by stacking unhewn stones (Ex 20:24-25). Many altars served as structures for sacrifices, such as the first altar referred to in Scripture, which was built by Noah after he and his family exited the ark. Later, Abraham built an altar of sacrifice on Mount Moriah, Manoah built an altar of sacrifice after an angel announced Samson's upcoming birth, and Elijah built an altar of sacrifice when he took on the prophets of Baal. While all of these were built for sacrifices, they would stand for years and become reminders of what God had done in those places.

Other altars were not built with the intention of sacrificing but were constructed simply to serve as a monument for remembrance. Take a minute to read Joshua 4:1-9.

Whose idea was it to build an altar?
How was the altar to be built?
Why was the altar to be built?

The altar on the west bank of the Jordan River would be a reminder to that generation and all who would follow of God's power and personal involvement in their lives. It would reduce the risk of spiritual amnesia.

A few years ago, I (Susan) was reading this account and became convicted that I needed to spend a few minutes building a few altars of remembrance. I didn't dare erect anything in our yard since Bentley is the one who usually mows, and if it's not concreted down, he will find a way to run the lawnmower smoothly over it. I decided instead to "build" my altars some-where I could run to them often and be reminded of God's involvement in my life, so I turned to the last blank page in my Bible and began drawing a small heap of rocks. I then began thinking of the times in my life when I had a sacred encounter with the living God and knew without a shadow of a doubt He was real and involved in my life. On top of that first heap of rocks, I drew a cookie and cup of Kool-Aid as a reminder of Vacation Bible School in 1977 when as an eight-year-old during snacks and recreation, I asked Jesus to take his rightful place as my Lord and Savior. On my second heap of rocks, I drew a worm to remind me of a time in my twenties when I was so overcome with the realization God was the Creator and I was the creature that it took me several minutes to be able to get out of my parked car. One of my favorite heaps of rocks has a sock on top of it with the following words written beside:

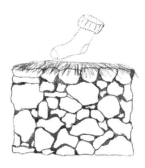

Fall '97: Still a little nervous about whether we could survive on a single income, I took a part-time job teaching Freshman Composition at the local college. I felt like God wanted me to be a full-time mom but was afraid we wouldn't be able to provide for our two children. I even cried to God, "But I want my children to always have socks and shoes." Within the week, a box of hand-me-downs arrived from twins in Houston. Inside were more socks than I could fit in my children's drawers. God made Himself clearly known as Jehovah Jireh, God the Provider.

More hand-drawn altars fill the last page of my Bible, one with a nail, reminding me of the time at a state evangelism con-ference when God helped me nail down my salvation to the point I have never doubted it again. Another is a drawing of an empty tomb, reminding me of the Easter I got a little excited about the resurrection during the special music and began to clap and cheer unexpectedly, scaring my poor husband and everyone around us. While these altars may seem simple to others, they mark times in my life when I knew God not only existed but cared.

Q&A: What are some of your spiritual milestones? In the space that follows (or on a blank page in your Bible), build a few altars of remembrance from your spiritual journey. Be sure to include your salvation, and be ready to share with one another the details of your salvation experience and other spiritual milestones.

Now that you have "built" these altars of remembrance, plan to visit them often, especially when trials come your way and cause you to question the goodness of God. Wrapping up this chapter, let's take a look at two Bible characters who made return trips to altars they had built.

In Genesis 12, the Lord instructs Abram to leave Haran and set out for Canaan. He arrives in Shechem where God promises to give Abram and his descendants the land he has passed through, and Abram commemorates the encounter with God with the first altar we find him building. Next, he journeys to Bethel where again he meets with God and builds an altar.

What happens to Abram in the last ten verses of Chapter 12?

Without God's direction or approval, Abram takes Sarai and heads out of the land God had promised him into the land of Egypt. This had negative consequences not only for Abram and Sarai but also for Pharaoh and his household. This, however, is where the story gets sweet.

According to Genesis 13:3, where does Abraham go next?

After surviving a near disaster, Abram goes back to the place where he had last been with God. It was the last place he had clearly heard the voice of God and knew He was real, so Abram went back to that altar at Bethel that served as a reminder that God cared and was personally involved in his life.

What a great example for us to follow. Whenever we find ourselves in a place that is unfamiliar and we're not sure what to do next, perhaps it's time to return to the last place where we clearly heard God speak to us and let Him begin leading again. That's what Abraham did, and it certainly proved beneficial.

Two generations later, we meet Abraham's grandson, Jacob. You remember him as the one who deceived his father and made his brother so angry that he had to escape to another country. Jacob was a man who not only distanced himself from his family but also from God. He was raised in a God-fearing home but refused to accept God personally. We find him constantly addressing God as the "God of my father Abraham and the God of my father Isaac." Then he has a personal encounter with God during a campout in Canaan.

According to Genesis 28:10-22, what does Jacob see in his dream?

What does God tell him in his dream?

What does Jacob call this place?

Jacob awakens and realizes that like his grandfather Abraham, he has received a promise from God. He is so moved by this divine encounter that he sets up a rock to mark the spot and basically tells God, "If you will give me food to eat and clothes to wear and take me back to my father's land someday, then you can be my God."

God not only provides for Jacob but blesses him immeasurably. Twenty years later as Jacob is making his way back home, God holds him to his word. The night before he will face Esau, Jacob spends a fitful, sleepless night wrestling with God, and as he wrestles he cries out, "Tell me your name." He was asking, "God, who are you? Tell me who you are. I know you are the God of my father Abraham and father Isaac, but who are you in relation to me?" This is a pivotal point for Jacob. For 40 years he has ridden on the faith of his forefathers; is this how he is going to live out the rest of his days? God sees Jacob's struggle and rewards him with a new name. He changes it from Jacob to Israel.

In response, Jacob gave God a new name. No longer did he refer to God as "the God of my fathers Abraham and Isaac," but look carefully at Genesis 33:20.

What new name did Jacob call God?

El Elohe Israel is translated "God, God of Israel." Jacob, now Israel, had found God to be his personal God and proclaimed him to be "God, God of Israel"—not the nation, but the person.

But the story is just beginning.

According to Genesis 35:1, where does God direct Jacob to settle?

What does God instruct him to do there?

So, our story has come full circle. Jacob returns to Bethel. No doubt he smiled when he came upon that first altar he had built where he had arrogantly made a deal with God. Now, he builds a second altar, naming it El Bethel, House of God. How sweet it must have been to revisit this place where God had made Himself personally known and to reflect on the way God had provided so lavishly for twenty long years.

Altars were never meant to be built and forgotten. God inspired them to be reminders of His faithfulness and love. As you discuss with one another the special places and times on your spiritual journey thus far, listen closely to the details of these encounters with God. It may be that in the days to come, you will be able to encourage one another by revisiting one of these altars and reminding one another that God is real and involved in your lives.

Keeping in Real with Nick and Samantha

We've often heard it said that the greatest gift you can bring into a relationship is a personal, growing, and thriving relationship with Christ. Sharing with one another how your spiritual journey began will not only grow you closer to one another, it will also grow you closer to God. It serves as a great reminder of what has brought you to seeking a God- honoring relationship in the first place.

Now is the perfect time to build a new altar, marking this moment as one where you commit your relationship with one another to be centered on Christ. You may want to consider finding a theme verse or a Christian song that will serve as a reminder of your commitment. From now on, keep each other accountable by bringing yourselves back to this altar that has set you apart as individuals and as a couple.

It's easy to set the relationship with God on the back burner as a new, romantic relationship begins to develop. Remember that He alone is your first love, and your relationship with Him should remain the priority. Now more than ever you will need to hear and to recognize God's voice. Be intentional about spending time together growing in the Lord, but also be vigilant in maintaining an individual quiet time so He can make His will known to you personally. Enjoy the journey.

Making the Most of Your Meaningful Conversation

1. What did you guess hippocampus to mean? On a scale from 1-10, how would you rate your hippocampus? Could you think of a time when you temporarily suffered from spiritual amnesia?

2. Which of the Scripture passages in this chapter did you find most interesting, encouraging, or enlightening?

3. When did you declare God as El Elohe of your life? Share your own salvation experience with one another. (Note: Guys, do more than tell the basic who, what, where, when, why, and how. Girls love to hear the details. Recall as many as you can.)

4. Show your "altars" to one another and share about these moments on your spiritual journey when you knew God to be real.

If during this chapter you realized that you have never had a personal encounter with God, know that you can today. Romans 10:9 promises, "That if you confess with your mouth, 'Jesus is Lord,' and believe in your heart that God raised him from the dead, you will be saved." The God of Abraham, Isaac, and Jacob wants to be El Elohe of your life, too. Invite Him to take his rightful place, share with another believer about your decision, and prepare to enjoy a life filled with purpose.

Chapter 2:

Prayer

Which of these best describes your prayer life?
   a) Hour of Power
   b) Land of Nod
   c) Phone a Friend
   d) Emergency 911

*A*sk any group of Christians what area of their spiritual walk needs more attention, and the most common answer will be prayer. While it has been easily defined as conversation with God, it is much more difficult to understand and practice. It is challenging to find the time to pray, and even when we do, we are a little uncertain as to how we go about this whole making our requests known business.

I (Bentley) remember turning 17 and thinking that it was probably time to begin praying about who would be my future spouse. My prayer often went something like this: "Lord, I'm a patient man. Take your time and prepare an incredible woman for me, and make me into the man who will be perfect for her." This prayer continued on through junior college, and as I entered a university, it changed slightly to, "Lord, I'm still a patient man. Settling down is on my mind a bit more these days, but I will wait for your timing, your woman. Feel free to introduce us anytime you see fit." This prayer sufficed for a couple of years. Then I found myself turning 22 and entering my last year of college, and pleading with God, "I'm not as patient as I used to be. Time is running out. Maybe perfection is overrated; I'll settle for breathing and semi-coherent." God is good. Despite my desperate prayers and willingness to settle, God honored the original prayers and sent me Susan.

While none of us would question that finding the perfect mate merits desperate praying, most of us realize that prayer is more than a begging session with God. It's about learning the heart of God and inviting His plan to be carried out. Even though we know this, we still find ourselves struggling with the discipline because of several misconceptions about prayer. As we take a look at five of these misconceptions, consider which ones have had the greatest impact on your life.

Misconceptions about Prayer

1. Prayer guarantees God will give me the desires of my heart.

Psalm 37:4 has found its way onto coffee mugs, prayer journals, and t-shirts, reminding the believer to "Delight yourself also in the LORD, and He shall give you the desires of your heart." This beautiful promise recorded by David has often been rearranged to say, "Pray to God about the desires of your heart, and he is delighted to give them to you." Big difference. This misinterpretation makes God out to be more of a genie in a lamp, waiting to be summoned and eager to grant our wishes. Aren't you glad He hasn't given you all your wishes?

In Numbers 11:15, Moses prays for God to "Kill me here and now." No doubt he was glad God didn't grant that desire of his heart expressed on a bad day.

Q&A: Can you think of a desire of your heart that you asked God for but are now glad He didn't grant?

David never meant for Psalm 37:4 to be a "name it and claim it" verse. It was his personal testimony that the more time he spent with the Lord, the more his desires were aligned to God's desires. Left on our own, Scripture indicates we will turn to evil desires (James 1:14). But as we spend moments delighting in God, He places a desire for righteousness in our hearts. For instance, God desires that all men come to him. As we spend time with God, He grows in our own hearts the desire to see others saved. God also desires His children live in unity. As we spend time delighting in God, we too develop a desire to do what we can to bring unity among the believers. Prayer is not about getting God to fulfill our desires; it is about letting Him instill His desires in our hearts to begin with. According to Scripture, prayer is about bending our will to align with God's rather than bending His will to align with ours.

If we pray under the misconception that prayer guarantees God will give us what we ask for, we set ourselves up for an unhealthy relationship with Him. The first time He doesn't give us what we want, we become angry with God and abandon prayer altogether. This often leads to the second misconception.

2. Prayer doesn't change anything.

Many of us hesitate to invest much time in prayer because we honestly wonder if it does any good. After all, God already knows what the future holds, so can we expect to change His mind or convince Him of anything through our prayers? Will our prayers change anything?

Perhaps Paul shared a bit of this same frustration. We read about a request he made in 2 Corinthians.

According to 2 Corinthians 12: 7-8, what did Paul pray about?

Does his prayer seem legitimate?

Did God change his situation?

On the surface, it appears that we could use this passage to prove that prayer doesn't change anything; however, I think Paul would quickly interject and argue that his fervent praying changed more than the situation; it changed the one praying. It was through his earnest pleading that God showed Paul His grace was sufficient, allowing Paul to later deliver that famous verse, "I can do all things through Christ who strengthens me" (Philippians 4:13). How much more powerful that statement is than "I can do all things through Christ who changes my situation." Paul found that prayer often changes the pray-er.

Another compelling example of this is found in Genesis 18. God told Abraham that the cities of Sodom and Gomorrah were being weighed in the balance, and judgment was about to rain down, literally. Abraham had a personal interest in these cities because his nephew, Lot, lived in Sodom, so Abraham began to pray about the situation: "Oh Lord, if you find 50 righteous people there, will you still sweep it away?" And God assures Abraham that if 50 righteous people are found, He'll spare the whole place. Then Abraham speaks up again, "What about 45, 40, 30, 20, 10?" And God assures him that even for the sake of 10, He would not destroy the city of Sodom. Many people will view these verses as a license to bargain with the Lord, God Almighty, but after a closer look at these verses, what we see is that Abraham is not just trying to bargain with God and convince Him to change the situation; Abraham is desperately trying to be at peace with whatever God's will might be in the situation. God is extremely patient with Abraham as he works through his fears and worries. You see, God is just as anxious for Abraham to be at peace with His sovereignty as Abraham is. Finally, Abraham has talked the situation over with God so thoroughly that he is completely convinced that God is going to do the right thing.

Did Abraham's prayer change the situation? Maybe not. Sodom and Gomorrah were still obliterated, but time spent in prayer did change Abraham. He was able to go home at peace with God. What if Abraham had stopped praying when he asked God about sparing Sodom for 20? He would have gone home a worried and fitful man. To stop a sentence short would have prevented the change that was most needed. Abraham was wise enough to know that prayer is about more than changing the situation; it's about changing the pray-er, and he stayed with it until he experienced the change and peace.

Both Paul and Abraham would gladly testify that prayer does indeed bring about change—sometimes in the situation, sometimes in the individual.

Q&A: Can you think of a time you prayed, and the situation didn't change, but somehow you did?

3. Prayer is for the old and super godly.

We were blessed to have a precious woman named Velma Deere as a part of our church family. Ms. Velma had been a widow for several years when we met her. She lived alone and spent hours each day loving on her animals, working in the flowers around her small A-frame house, and reading the Word of God. We knew Ms. Velma's prayer life was an extraordinary one because sometimes she would be having a conversation with us and smoothly transition right into a conversation with God. We became bystanders for the next few minutes as the 86-year-old updated the Lord on various situations, and then shifted just as smoothly back into a dialogue with us. It was always fun to see someone experience this for the first time with Ms. Velma. Most folks would look around to see if perhaps someone else had arrived on the scene; others would try to figure out if they should bow their heads or consider the conversation finished.

We often found ourselves envying Ms. Velma's prayer life. It seemed to come as naturally for her as her next breath. Although she never wrote a book or delivered a sermon, she should be classified with other great men and women of prayer like Martin Luther who spent at least two hours in prayer each day and E.M. Bounds who started each day at 4 with three hours of prayer. Of course, we can't forget George Mueller who never asked for a penny but whose prayers resulted in millions of dollars to care for over 10,000 orphans.

As we read accounts about people like Ms. Velma, Luther, Bounds, and Mueller, it is easy to buy into the misconception that prayer is for the old and super godly. Perhaps we figure that, unlike us, they have the time or understanding to possess powerful prayer lives, but nowhere in Scripture do we find that a certain age or a certain amount of time is required to have an effective prayer life. Neither do we find that a certain level of spiritual maturity must be reached before a great prayer life can be achieved. Instead, we find the common denominator among great men and women of prayer is they were intentional about praying. It seems prayer is a pre-requisite for spiritual maturity rather than spiritual maturity being a pre-requisite for prayer.

Perhaps this is why the disciples asked Jesus to teach them *to pray* rather than *how to pray*. They understood their greatest hindrance to a powerful prayer life was not praying wrong; it was not praying at all.

According to James 4:2, what is at the heart of our ineffective prayer lives?

When we convince ourselves that prayer is for the older, wiser, and more godly, we will disqualify ourselves and miss out on the fellowship and blessings that God desires to share with us. This is both a shame and a sin.

Read James 4:17. If we know we are to pray, and we choose not to, what does James indicate?

Another Scripture both convicting and inspiring is found in the Old Testament book of 1 Samuel. The children of Israel had asked for a king, and through the prophet Samuel, God anointed Saul. At the official coronation, the people ask Samuel to continue to be their advocate before a Holy God. In the space below, record Samuel's reply in 1 Samuel 12:23.

God calls us to pray, and to fail to do so is actually considered disobedience and sin, but developing a dynamic prayer life is not easy. It is hard work. One college student lamented, "It is easier for me to spend ten hours in Bible study that one hour in fervent prayer." Regardless of how hard it is, we must pray if we want to please God.

Paul gives some sound instruction on how to do this. In one of the shortest verses in the Bible, he simply says, "Pray without ceasing" (1 Thessalonians 5:17). Paul is encouraging us to realize that prayer is not simply two to four hours set aside at the beginning of the day; prayer must become our lifestyle. As we work, study, play, and relate to others, we pray. And as we do, we will discover that prayer is not just for the old and super godly; it is for the individual who longs to please God.

Q&A: Who do you know that you consider a prayer warrior, and why do you see him or her in this role?

4. *Prayer should leave me feeling invigorated.*

Sometimes it will. Remember the prayer meeting that is recorded in Acts 4:23-31? Earlier in the chapter, Peter and John were arrested for speaking healing into the life of a 40-year-old lame man and then preaching about Christ who made the healing possible. Upon their release from prison, Peter and John returned to their compadres, shared all that had happened, and a spontaneous prayer meeting broke loose.

According to Acts 4:31, what happened as the people prayed?

No doubt, that was a prayer meeting those folks talked about for the rest of their lives, but do you think that the earth shook and the Spirit moved in such a visible way every time they prayed? It would be safe to say more often than not, their prayers were met with much less dramatic results. How easy it would have been for this group of new Christians to grow weary in their prayer lives if they had compared all of their prayer meetings to the Acts 4 one.

We can learn an important lesson from that early church. While some prayer times will energize and invigorate us, others will be less than earth shaking. In fact, Scripture indicates that earnest prayer can make us feel

- Broken (Nehemiah 1:4),
- Exhausted (1 Kings 19:5),
- Humbled (Isaiah 6:5-6), and
- Challenged beyond our abilities (Matthew 17:14-21).

This will greatly frustrate us if we are under the misconception that prayer should always leave us feeling exhilarated, or at least warm and fuzzy. Many of the college students we work with become disheartened, feeling that their prayers are simply bouncing off the ceiling. We remind them that these are the crucial moments when God calls on them to act on what they know instead of what they feel.

I consider Patrice to be a dear friend and spiritual adviser. She has invested her life in mentoring young women in the beautiful backwoods of Southeast Oklahoma, and has taught incredible lessons on everything from marriage to ministry, but the loudest lesson I have ever heard her teach was in a one-on-one conversation with her during a challenging season in her life. She described feeling frustrated because her once powerful times of prayer now felt more like a one-sided conversation. Then Patrice said something I will never forget. "You know what I'm doing?" she asked. "Every morning, I sit down in my quiet spot, and I tell God, 'I'm here. Whether you speak to me today or not, I'm here, and I'm going to read your Word, and I'm going to pray. I would love for You to show up today, but even if You don't, I'm here.'"

That, my friend, is spiritual maturity. Patrice's prayer life was based on the truth that God had invited her to come before Him in prayer, and she was going to rest on that truth rather than any feeling. She called that season of her life the "silent months," and rest assured they built incredible character in this already godly woman.

Like Patrice, we must understand that just because God is silent doesn't mean He is inactive. Mrs. Charles E. Cowman, in her devotional *Streams in the Desert,* recounts an old tale of a Christian who through a dream watched three women in prayer. As they prayed, Christ drew near. He approached the first woman, knelt beside her, and lavished her with love and words of affirmation. Then he moved to the second woman and gently laid his hand on her head and smiled. When he came to the third, he hardly acknowledged her and continued to walk past without a word or a touch. The dreaming woman tried desperately to interpret what she had seen. She decided the first woman must be a delight to Christ because of the way He showed such obvious approval and affection. The second woman must be making spiritual progress because she, too, gained the Master's attention. And the third woman must have done something that distanced herself from God since she didn't merit so much as a nod of acknowledgement.

Then God spoke to the dreaming Christian and said, "O woman. How wrongly has thou interpreted Me. The first kneeling woman needs all the weight of My tenderness and care to keep her feet in My narrow way. She needs My love, thought, and help every moment of the day. Without it, she would fail and fall. The second has a stronger faith and deeper love, and I can trust her to trust Me however things may go and whatever people do. The third, whom I seemed not to notice and even to neglect, has faith and love of the finest quality, and her I am training by quick and drastic processes for the highest and holiest service."

It was this third praying woman who would be faithful to pray, even when God seemed silent and prayer invoked no feeling. She had not fallen for the misconception prayer should always leave us feeling invigorated. The truth is sometimes God does his greatest work during the silence. Think about the cross. Here, God did his greatest work of all time, but to everyone around, it must have seemed He was being extremely silent. Prayers were offered by the Son, prayers were offered by His followers, but because God was quiet, don't think for a minute He wasn't busy. It was during this silence He was doing His most intricate work and making a way for all mankind to be saved.

Maybe your prayer life has been less than exciting. Don't buy into the lie that all prayers will leave you singing "I Saw the Light." Even if those prayers seem to be bouncing off the ceiling, keep praying, trusting God is active regardless of what you are feeling.

Q&A: Can you recall a powerful time of prayer you have experienced?

Can you recall a time when your prayer life was anything but exciting?

5. Prayer is the preparation for God's work.

We pray before meals. We pray before making a big decision. We pray before ball games, surgeries, mission trips, and hard tests. If we aren't careful, we begin to believe prayer is simply a preliminary event, the preparation for God's work. Prayer is much more. Oswald Chamber once wrote, "Prayer does not equip us for greater works—prayer is the greater work." It is in those moments on our knees God does His greatest work.

Let's see if we can prove this through Scripture. Maybe you remember the story of a young Jewish orphan who won a royal beauty contest and was named Queen of Persia. Esther's testimony is about as action-packed as they come with assassination attempts, romance, irony, and redemption, but what if you had to pinpoint the highlight of Esther's reign? What would you declare as her finest hour? Some may say it was that moment when she donned her royal robes, risked her life, and stood before King Xerxes on behalf of the Jewish nation.

Others may say it was in Chapter 7 when she is sitting at the table with the King and pleads with him to spare the Jews and deal with Haman. A few would even point to the end of the story and declare the climax of her time as royalty was when she witnessed her people celebrating their deliverance from annihilation and victory over their enemies.

All of these were incredible moments in Esther's life, but it is entirely possible that Queen Esther's finest hour took place before any of these great events occurred.

Look closely at Esther 4:16. Why might this be considered Esther's finest hour?

Perhaps Queen Esther's finest hour was not dressed in royal robes before King Xerxes or standing as a national hero before the Jews. Perhaps Queen Esther's finest hour was spent on her knees. Note that she did not spend three days in prayer trying to decide whether to go to the king with her request; she had already decided it must be done. Instead, those three days were spent making sure her heart was pure before the King of Creation before she ever approached the King of Persia. She knew her need to seek a higher throne before approaching a lesser one, and she invited all of the Jews in the capital city of Susa to join her in doing so. What transpired in those three days was absolutely critical in determining what would happen in the days and months that followed. For Esther, prayer was not the preparation for great works; it was the great work, her finest hour.

The same could be said of one of her contemporaries, Nehemiah. He is often remembered as the Jewish layman who led the rebuilding project in Jerusalem. He must have had some incredible moments like the twenty-fifth day of Elul when the wall was declared completed in a miraculous 52 days or the dedication ceremony where two large thanksgiving choirs sang and walked on the wall that enemies had said even a fox could break down. However, if we asked Nehemiah when his finest hour occurred, I think he would take us back to Chapter 1.

According to Nehemiah 1:4, what did Nehemiah do when he first heard about the condition of Jerusalem?

Nehemiah was not preparing for God's work during those many days of prayer; he was doing the greatest work. He was genuinely searching for the heart of God so that the prayer he offered in 1:5-11 and every activity that followed would be in tune with God. As you read Chapter 1, you will notice that Nehemiah spent more time searching for the heart of God than making the actual request, but when he did, he could do so boldly because he knew his heart was pure and his motives were right.

And so we see prayer is much more than preparation for God's work; it *is* God's work. It is where the relationship is matured and finest hours are born.

As was mentioned earlier in this chapter, prayer is hard work, but it is certainly some of the most rewarding work you will ever do. Recognizing and confronting these five misconceptions is a great way to begin your journey toward a healthier prayer life.

As you prepare to talk about prayer with one another, spend a few minutes in honest evaluation about your current prayer life. Chances are you will both see room for improvement, so don't try to impress one another; be honest and transparent. Realize God never intended prayer to be a guilt trip. Rather, it is both a great calling and high privilege.

Also, spend a few minutes praying specifically for the person with whom you are doing this study. You may want to list below some of the specific requests you are making on behalf of that person.

"And pray in the Spirit on all occasions with all kinds of prayers and requests. With this in mind, be alert and always keep on praying for all the Lord's people." Ephesians 6:18 (NIV)

Keeping it Real with Nick and Samantha

The greatest dating relationships (and eventually marriages) are those in which a couple feels comfortable praying for one another and with one another. What does this look like for the dating couple?

1. *Pray for wisdom in your relationship.* Ask God to show you how you can best respect and treat the other person. Ask Him to help you avoid temptations. Ask Him how to best keep the relationship Christ-centered. (If you're reading this book, you're off to a great start.)
2. *Pray that you might fulfill your God-given responsibility to the relationship and to your boyfriend/girlfriend.* In 1 Thessalonians 5:11, we are instructed to encourage one another and build each other up. Ask God for opportunities to do this for one another.
3. *Pray for various situations and people outside of your relationship.* It is easy to get caught up in each other and forget about the outside world. Pray together for missions, your families, your churches, items in the news, or a specific cause.
4. *Pray throughout the date, but especially at the end of each date.* We found that by doing so, we were able to avoid compromising situations.

Time spent in prayer is always time well spent. It will do much to grow a person and a relationship.

Making the Most of Your Meaningful Conversation

1. Which phrase at the beginning of the chapter did you choose to describe your prayer life and why?

2. Can you think of a desire of your heart you asked God for but you are now glad He didn't grant?

3. Can you think of a time you prayed and the situation didn't change, but somehow you did?

4. Who do you know that you consider a prayer warrior, and why do you see him or her in this role?

5. Can you recall a powerful time of prayer you have experienced?

6. Have you experienced a season when it felt like your prayers were bouncing off the ceiling? What did you learn during this time?

7. How might it change our prayer lives if we really believed that prayer is not the preparation for God's work but is God's work?

8. Of the five misconceptions discussed, which one has had the greatest effect on your prayer life?

9. What might God be asking you to do to improve your prayer life?

10. What is at least one thing for which you would appreciate prayer at this point in your life?

Chapter 3:

Fear

Rank the following in order, based on your own fears: 1= greater fear, 5= lesser fear.

_____ Yard gnomes
_____ Public speaking
_____ Spiders, snakes, and scorpions
_____ Walking alone at night
_____ The dentist

*F*ear is a complicated emotion. Part of our chemical makeup enjoys a good scare from a horror movie or exhilarating ride. Another part avoids at all cost anything that might make our heart race and pits sweat. Fear and people's reactions to it remain a mystery to even the most credible psychologists who are now classifying it as a disease. It may or may not be contagious, but it can certainly generate symptoms such as nausea, headaches, and dizziness and even put us at risk for low immunity, heart disease, or cancer. Fear of some kind will land more than 25 million Americans in a doctor's office this year where they will be diagnosed with anxiety disorders that range from panic attacks to one of the more than 100 phobias which now have been identified and given names.

Most of us are familiar with the more common phobias such as claustrophobia (fear of small spaces) and hemophobia (fear of blood). Others are common, but their medical names are less well known, aerophobia (fear of flying) and astraphobia (fear of thunder and lightning), for example. While only a select few have probably dealt with alektorophobia (fear of chickens), most of us would have to admit to suffering from monophobia (fear of being alone) or xenophobia (fear of the unknown) at some point in our lives. After reading the last paragraph, we probably all now suffer from

Hippopotomonstrosesquipedaliophobia (fear of long words).

An important truth in dealing with fears is to realize some fears are simply unfounded. In fact, they can seem downright comical. Yard gnomes, for instance. Yes, they look a little creepy, but they are made of concrete. They absolutely cannot come to life and watch us with those beady little eyes.

When our kids were younger, we would reward good grades with an outing to a family-friendly pizza place filled with games, rides, and stage shows. Life was always good until a larger-than-life costumed mouse made his appearance and attempted to high five and shake hands with the over-caffeinated munchkins. Our daughter could spot him from any ride and two rooms away. She would make a mad dash for our booth, pushing down any kids who got in her way, and seek refuge under the table until we assured her the mouse had returned to his cage in the kitchen. Time and again we tried to help her overcome her fear of the friendly rodent; time and again she reminded us that no mouse should ever be that big.

Q&A: *Think back to your own childhood. Did you have any silly fears that now you are able to laugh about?*

We expect children to be afraid of unusual objects or circumstances, but what about adults? Are we sometimes unnecessarily afraid? I (Susan) do not have an adventurous bone in my body. I love dreaming about climbing Mount Everest, canoeing through the Amazon, or bungee jumping in the Grand Canyon, but take me to an amusement park, and the carousel is about as wild as I get. I'm not sure if I suffer from acrophobia (fear of heights) or emetophobia (fear of vomiting). Either way, I always carry a large camera around and use it as my excuse for being unable to enjoy the rides. Most of the time, I don't feel like I'm missing out on a thing, but one year our family took a vacation to the Rocky Mountains of Colorado. Everyone was abuzz with plans to go white water rafting. We had several children along, so calls were made to find the mildest expedition. A vote was taken, and reservations were made for a Class II adventure.

I remained silent during the decision-making process, trying to come up with a good excuse to avoid the whole situation. My kids, reading my mind, showed me the assuaging brochure that promised "easy rapids with smaller waves, clear channels that are obvious without scouting." As my kids begged, I realized I didn't want them to grow up with memories of mom as the fuddy-dud, so I decided to walk on the wild side and ordered my ticket. Later that night as I was begging God for courage, I made the mistake of looking back over the brochure, and for the first time, my eyes went to the small print that read, "Some maneuvering might be required." It might as well have said, "You will encounter ginormous waterfalls and hazardous rapids."

I may have slept for two hours that night as I played out in my mind all the things that could go wrong and desperately hoped for a sudden case of chicken pox to get me out of the trip altogether. By 10:00 A.M., however, I was being buckled into a life jacket that seemed too loose and shoved into a raft that seemed too flimsy. While the rest of the family laughed and joked, I prayed both silently and out loud as we shoved away from the shore. As we floated, enjoying the beauty of the towering spruce trees and snow-capped mountains, I found myself releasing the death grip I had on the rope. I still gritted my teeth the first time the river picked up pace and a little water splashed into my face. By the second little "rapid," I was able to keep my eyes open and even grin a bit. Thirty minutes and two rapids later, I was waving my oar in the air like a mad-woman and singing "Bad to the Bone." Later that night back in the room, my daily devotion was taken from Psalm 53:5 which read, "There they are in great fear where no fear was." How appropriate. It had been an incredible day, and I had almost let fear keep me from enjoying the day with my family.

While I'm still not ready to jump on a roller coaster or sky-dive from an airplane, God taught me an important lesson that day. Sometimes I can let my imagination run away with me and become extremely anxious about something that is not that big of a deal. Many times I am simply filled with fear when there is nothing to fear. Whether I am tackling a new project, making a phone call, or visiting the dentist, sometimes fear will make a situation seem worse in my mind than the experience itself could ever be. If I don't recognize this negative tendency, fear will prevent me from enjoying some of life's most breathtaking moments and cause me to wrestle with unnecessary stress.

Q&A: What about you? When was the last time you feared or dreaded something only to find out there was nothing to fear or dread?

While some fears are unwarranted, there are situations and circumstances that certainly merit a cautious attitude. Folks living in coastal states develop a healthy respect for hurricane advisories, just as those of us in the Midwest take seriously the piercing wail of a tornado siren. It is no surprise that survivors of such natural disasters develop lilaspsophobia (the fear of tornadoes and hurricanes). Some situations present a legitimate concern and naturally strike a chord of fear in our hearts.

Q&A: *Do you have a legitimate fear? Is there something that happened to make this a real fear in your life?*

Matthew records one such situation in 8:23-27 as he describes a late evening voyage across the Sea of Galilee.

According to Matthew 8:24, how intense was the storm at sea?

These disciples didn't sign up for a Class VI whitewater rafting adventure. They simply followed Christ into the boat and were obeying Him by escorting Him across the lake. This sure blows the theory that following Christ will always be smooth sailing right out of the water. Sometimes we can be right in the center of God's will and still find ourselves in the middle of a raging storm.

The storm these disciples faced that evening was a doozy; the waves were sweeping over the boat. We know there must have been a legitimate concern because even the seasoned fishermen aboard the boat who had survived tempests before were crying out in desperation. Most of us would agree this was a crisis situation, and what are we taught to do when faced with a crisis? Take it to Jesus—pray. That's exactly what these disciples did. They took their concern to the One who could do something about it. They didn't get together and form a committee on squall control. They did exactly what they should have—they called out to their Savior. If the disciples were in the right place and they did the right thing, then why does Jesus reprimand them so harshly in verse 28 when He asks, "Why are you fearful, O you of little faith?" Why did Jesus point out their lack of faith when they had sought Him?

Scripture unveils the answer beginning in Chapter 8. A few days earlier, Christ encountered a leper. What incredible statement of faith did the leper make in Matthew 8:2?

Jesus was pleased with the prayer of this leper. There was no bargaining and pleading. No justification as to why the miracle was necessary. No threats if a miracle was not delivered. Just a simple prayer of faith: "You are able; are you willing?" It appears that even if the healing had not come, even if Jesus had replied, "The time is not right," this man would still have maintained his faith in Christ. It was a settled issue before he ever approached the Lord.

This leper's faith reminds us of three Hebrew men who were faced with a dilemma of their own. King Nebuchadnezzar had sentenced them to the fiery furnace, but before they were thrown into that pit, they calmly professed, "Our God whom we serve is able to deliver us from the burning fiery furnace, and He will deliver us from your hand, O king. But if not, let it be known to you, O king, that we do not serve your gods, nor will we worship the gold image you have set up" (Dan 3:17-18). No moment of panic. No cries for mercy. Like the leper, these three men were convinced God was able to remedy their crisis; there was no question about whether He could, and they were all willing to accept whatever He decided to do.

God delivered those faithful Hebrew men out of the flames, and Jesus was willing to heal the leper. He made the leper clean and sent him to show the priest, and then a few miles down the road, Jesus ran into a Roman centurion who also had a crisis.

Take a moment to read Matthew 8:5-13. According to verse 6, what legitimate concern did the centurion have?

The centurion approached Jesus with a fear-filled situation, and Scripture says Jesus "marveled" at the way he did so. This man, who was not even a Jew- he was a Roman centurion, an enemy of the Jews- astonishes Christ with his prayer. Why? The answer lies in verse 8. The centurion has already told Jesus the problem, and Jesus has already agreed to go and take care of it. The centurion doesn't have to beg, plead, or bargain any more. Christ has already said OK. But listen to what the centurion says next: "Lord, I do not deserve to have you come under my roof, but just say the word..."

You see, the Jews recognized that Jesus had power. They knew that His touch had healed many, but this centurion knew that the power was not in His touch but in His authority which came from on high. It was not some kind of hocus pocus but the real deal that came from being one with God. The centurion's understanding of the identity of Jesus Christ made it possible for him to declare, "Look, I know who you are. With a word you spoke the world into existence, and with a word you can heal my servant." This kind of faith, coming from a man who was not even brought up in a traditional Jewish home, astonished and delighted our Lord.

Now, think about something: Where were the disciples when Jesus was having these conversations with the leper and the centurion? They were right there. The disciples had witnessed these two incredible testimonies of faith days, maybe even hours, before they got in that boat with Christ, yet when they were faced with a crisis of their own, what was their response? "Lord, save us! We're drowning! Don't you even care?"

Fear outweighed faith in the hearts of the disciples in their predicament at sea. They did seek out Christ, which was a good thing, but they did so in a state of panic. How much more pleased would Christ have been if their response had been that of the leper and the centurion whom they had encountered earlier? Instead of yelling, "Save us! Don't you care?" what if they had awakened him with the words, "Lord, you are able. If you are willing, just speak the word." Perhaps instead of issuing a reprimand, Christ could have marveled at their faith and commended their reaction.

The disciples still got what they wanted, even with their panicky prayer, but how much more incredible that experience might have been if after He told the waters and the wind, "Peace, be still," He could have turned to those disciples and said, "Well done. It is good to see such great faith right here in Israel."

Like the disciples, we will face some fear-filled storms. Will we let our fear outweigh our faith? Many people have tried to define faith, but the best definition we have run across defines faith as the refusal to panic. It's not that a believer is never to be scared. Some situations present legitimate concerns. But Christ is honored when we refuse to panic because we know Who He is, what He is able to do, and trust that He will do what is right. I John tells us that God is love and that perfect love casts out fear. It stands to reason that as our faith matures, there will be less room for fear that makes us panic.

Q&A: *What is typically your first reaction in a moment of fear? Do you scream, shake, run, freeze? What would you like for your first reaction to be?*

Perhaps one of the reasons God addresses fear so frequently in Scripture is because He knows that fear left unchecked can control us. Consider the Pharisees. One of the main reasons the chief priests, scribes, and elders of Jesus's day opposed Him was because He was drawing attention and could rock the boat with the Romans whose jurisdiction they were under. They enjoyed what little power the Romans had given them and feared that it could be taken away if a problem arose among the Jews who were entrusted in their watch-care. What else do you learn about this group of Jewish leaders from the following verses?

Mark 11:18

Mark 11: 27-33

Mark 12:12

These men were afraid of everyone and everything. Their fear controlled them; as a result, so did everyone who crossed their path. Talk about a miserable way to live.

Perhaps the main reason God addresses fear so frequently is because He knows that when we are controlled by fear, we miss out on the opportunity to have a Divine encounter with

Him. This was certainly true for the Pharisees, priests and scribes. The God they professed to serve was standing before them in the flesh, and because of fear, they missed Him.

The disciples provide another perfect example. They didn't do well on their first faith test on the Sea of Galilee, so some time later, Jesus took them back to that same body of water for a do-over. He sent them on across to Bethsaida while He spent time talking with His Father, probably praying the disciples would get it right this time. Then Jesus did what only He can and began walking across the tumultuous waters.

According to Matthew 14:25-26, how did the disciples respond to a fear-filled situation this time?

Same sea, same waves, same response; however, Peter quickly recovers, allows faith to overcome his fear, and takes Jesus up on the invitation of a lifetime. It wasn't that Peter was extraordinarily courageous; within a few more chapters, he completely denies knowing Christ. Even in this moment, the waves and wind were terrifying, but Peter saw Christ on those waves, and his desire to be with Jesus was greater than his fear of the impossible. In an incredible act of faith, he stepped out on those waves because that was where Christ was, and where Christ was, was where Peter wanted to be. Granted, that fear soon returned, but at least for a moment, he had a Divine encounter and did what no other man was willing to try or has ever done since. Could the other disciples have experienced the same thing? Sure, but their fear kept them in the boat, watching the Divine encounter at a distance.

Q&A: Has fear ever kept you from doing something you now wish you had?

We find a similar situation in Exodus 19. The children of Israel have been out of Egypt for three months, and they have witnessed some pretty incredible events during those ninety days: the parting of the Red Sea, bitter water turned sweet, manna and quail from heaven, water from a rock, and a victory over the Amalekites, not to mention having the first GPS—a cloud that led them where they needed to go. Now, that cloud has led them into the desert and to the base of Mount Sinai. Moses goes to the top of the mountain, and God tells them that in three days He's going to come down on Mount Sinai in the sight of all the people. Moses returns and helps the people get ready for the big event. Can you imagine what must have been going through those folks' minds? Whatever it was they expected, they certainly got more.

According to Exodus 19:16-19, what did the people see, hear, and experience?

What an amazing sight. Thunder and lightning, smoke and fire, dark clouds and a shaking mountain. It was as if they were experiencing a volcano, earthquake, and fierce thunderstorm all at one time. Then there was the trumpet without a trumpeter in sight. The last part of verse 16 tells us "all the people who were in the camp trembled." I bet they did. Before, they had seen the miracles of God, but God was inviting them to take this relationship to a whole new level. He was making Himself known in a new way. When they thought it couldn't get any more exciting or terrifying, they began to hear the voice of God. Can you imagine what it must have been like to see and to hear the God of all creation displaying His glory, making Himself recognizable in a big way? It's not surprising that God would make Himself known, but it is surprising how the people reacted.

According to Exodus 20:18-19, what was the people's reaction?

Here, you find people who are getting to see God in a way that no one else ever had before, and how do they respond? "We can't take it. It's too much. We're uncomfortable and more than a little afraid, to say the least." The KJV tells us "They removed and stood afar off." Is that what God wanted? Earlier He had set boundaries and told the people not even to touch the mountain until the ram's horn sounded a long blast, but those boundaries did not seem to have even been needed. We don't see anyone pressing forward to get a closer look, no one working through the crowd to be closer to the God who had brought them out of bondage. Instead, we find them backing up. They even turned to Moses and said, "You speak with us, and we will hear; but let not God speak with us, lest we die." In other words, "Moses, you go find out what God has to say. We'll stay right here and be content to hear it from you." These people let fear keep them at a distance and settled for secondhand information when they had the opportunity to enjoy a Divine encounter with God.

Maybe we are not so different today. When it comes to God, the majority of people seem to be satisfied to stand at a distance and receive secondhand information from God. It's okay to go to church on Sunday morning and fill a pew. That's a good, safe distance. We will let the pastor go get the message and bring it back to us. If the message is applicable to our lives, great. If not, at least we were there showing reverence and respect. But God wants more than our reverence and respect. He wants a relationship. The Israelites standing at the foot of Mt. Sinai showed reverence and respect, but because of fear, they missed out on that relationship. We will, too, if we let fear control us and are satisfied to stand at a distance and receive secondhand information. This is where Moses becomes the role model for how to face fear.

According to Exodus 20:20-21, how does Moses handle this nerve-wracking, fear-packing situation?

Moses saw the same dark cloud, lightning, and fire. He heard the same thunder and trumpet blasts. He felt the same trembling mountain. Verse 21, however, tells us that while the people remained at a distance, Moses "approached the thick darkness where God was." Moses didn't know what he would find when he entered that dark cloud; it looked like a volcano. He wasn't sure if it might cost him his life. He only knew that was where God was, and where God was is where Moses wanted to be.

When our daughter was five and our son was three, we took a family vacation to Eureka Springs, Arkansas, to see the Passion Play. We had been building it up, telling the kids how we would get to see Mary, the disciples, and Jesus. Finally, the evening arrived, and we joined in the steady stream of traffic filling the parking lot. Once we parked, I (Susan) unbuckled Samantha, set her outside the door, and turned to unbuckle Brent. Samantha took off across that parking lot, darting between rolling cars and running as fast as her legs would carry her. Fortunately, Bentley's legs were longer, and he finally caught her. He brought her back to the car, and we began giving her the lecture about how she could have been run over. She looked up at us with big brown eyes and matter-of-factly explained, "But guys, I'm going to see Jesus! I gotta go see Jesus!"

That is a Moses mentality. No matter what the cost, I must see Him. No matter how dark the cloud, I'm going in. No matter how real the fear, my desire to be with God is stronger. From Exodus 20 to Deuteronomy 34, we find Moses going back up that mountain again and again. In fact, our last glimpse of Moses is of him climbing Mount Nebo. Why? Because that was where God was, and as scary as that climb might have been, where God was, was where Moses wanted to be.

Q&A: Do you have any fears that are keeping you standing at a distance rather than experiencing God first hand?

Fear is a powerful emotion. In its proper place, it can actually be a good thing and keep us from taking risks that are neither wise nor helpful. A healthy dose of catapedaphobia (fear of jumping from high places) will keep us all from becoming tightrope walkers over Niagara Falls. A little ophidiophobia (fear of snakes) might spare us from a wrestling match with a venom-filled viper. In these instances, fear is good and necessary for the survival of humankind.

But as we have seen in Scripture, fear also can be negative when it paralyzes us and prevents us from doing what we know is right. In John 10:10, Christ reminded His folllowers that He came "that they may have life, and that they may have it more abundantly." It's impossible for us to live that abundant life when we are controlled by fear. The abundant life is one lived in faith rather than fear, and God reminds us through one story after another, "Don't panic; just trust."

Following Him will not always seem safe. There may be some pretty nerve-wracking, fear-packing moments. But when our desire to experience God is greater than our fears and our phobias, something supernatural is sure to happen. Don't let those fears control you like the Pharisees. Don't stay in the boat when a divine encounter awaits. Brave the rogue waves like Peter, approach the thick darkness like Moses, because where He is, is where you want to be.

"For God has not given us a spirit of fear, but of power and of love and of a sound mind." 2 Timothy 1:7

Keeping it Real with Nick and Samantha

Samantha: After we had been dating for about five months, Nick went on a mission trip to Southeast Asia. During those 19 days apart, I was overwhelmed with fear of the team getting caught, for Christianity was not encouraged in the area they were serving. They could have been deported, imprisoned, or even worse. Helplessness consumed me. It finally occurred to me that I could spend three weeks a stressed mess or a blessed interceder. The latter sounded much more attractive, and I learned to convert my fears for Nick's safety into prayers for him, a lesson that has benefited us much in marriage.

Nick: Fear can be an overwhelming emotion if the promises of God are forgotten. In China, my team and I found ourselves in a helpless situation. The local Communist Party was getting suspicious of our late night activities of sneaking into hotel rooms and smuggling Bibles in at 2 A.M. Our translators were Chinese believers and had to leave town in a hurry to avoid being associated with us. This left us teaching English to Chinese students, without help from translators, in a foreign country where it was illegal to share our faith. The easy thing to do? Go home and be safe. The hard thing to do? Stay and share our faith boldly. God promises He will never leave or forsake us (Heb 13:5). He also says our work for Him is never in vain (1 Cor 15:58). Through our team's darkest nights in China, God was always faithful. His promises and provisions have never been more physically visible in my life than when He got our team out of Southeast Asia, safe and sound.

Making the Most of Your Meaningful Conversation

1. How did you rank the fears listed at the beginning of this chapter?

2. Can you think of a time someone got a good scare in on you?

3. Did you have any silly fears as a child that you are now able to laugh about?

4. When was the last time you feared or dreaded something only to find out there was nothing to fear or dread?

5. How about a legitimate fear? Is there something that has happened to make this a real fear in your life?

6. What is typically your first reaction in a moment of fear? Do you scream, shake, run, freeze? What would you like for your first reaction to be?

7. Peter's water walking story is a familiar one. What do you think are the most important details of it and the greatest lesson to be learned?

8. Has fear ever kept you from doing something you now wish you had?

9. Based on Exodus 19-20, describe Moses in one word.

10. Do you have any fears that are keeping you standing at a distance rather than experiencing God first hand?

Chapter 4:

Entertainment

The ideal date might include
    a) dinner and a movie.
    b) greasy pizza and a sporting event.
    c) listening to the radio while fishing.
    d) a day at the amusement park/zoo followed by ice cream.
    e) other: _____

*T*hose of us living in the 21st Century love to be entertained. The newest house plans include theater rooms and back yards occupied by salt-water swimming pools; vacation travel is at an all-time high. In 2014, movie goers spent 10.44 billion dollars at the box office, which was slightly down from the year before, probably because we were spending nearly 18 billion dollars on home entertainment rentals and sales.[1]

According to a 2015 Fox News article, Americans spend more money eating out than buying groceries, a first in history, amounting to an estimated 1.8 billion dollars every day.[2] And here's a real shocker: the latest statistics published by Fox News estimate the average date costs $100…that's more than many of us make for a day's work.[3]

We are not only investing more *money* in the entertainment industry but also investing more *time* in the industry. In

2013, the average American 15 and older spent 35 hours a week on leisure and sports time entertainment (watching TV by far the most popular), almost equating it to the time spent in a full-time job.[4] It seems our culture's mantra has become "Work Hard; Play Harder." We justify the money and time spent by declaring there's nothing wrong with having fun, and this is true. An evening spent at the ballpark with the family can be a healthy recreational activity. Movies inspire and vacations make memories. In fact, some of our sweetest memories probably involve some form of entertainment.

Q&A: *What is one of your favorite entertainment related memories?*

Entertainment itself is not a bad thing; however, with all the choices available, it has become increasingly imperative for individuals who truly desire to glorify God to set some God-honoring standards in the arena of entertainment.

Take a moment to read 1 Corinthians 10:31. Do you believe this applies to your entertainment choices?
YES   NO   Why or why?

It appears Paul is challenging his audience to live lives that glorify God in every aspect, including food, drink, and entertainment. He challenges his readers (including us) to seek to live lives of integrity. I (Susan) have to be honest; until a few years ago, I wasn't sure what this word meant, so I began a study and found that the word *integrity* comes from the Hebrew word *tom*. Much to my surprise, the word is used repeatedly in Scripture. I thought integrity was a word made popular by the Promise Keepers movement, but it is actually a God-original. The first time we find it used in Scripture is in Genesis 20. Here, we find the story of Abraham and Sarah who have moved to the region of Gerar and told everyone in town they are brother and sister because Abraham is afraid if the men know Sarah is his wife, they might kill him in order to marry her. Because of their partial lie (they actually were half brother and sister; check it out in Genesis 20:12), the King of Gerrar, a man named Abimelech, decides to claim Sarah for his own. Fortunately, God comes to Abimelech in a dream and tells him Sarah is a married woman, and he is as good as dead for having taken her.

Look closely at Abimelech's reply in Genesis 20:4-5. How did he describe himself to God?

In the original Hebrew text, the phrase "clear conscience and clean hands" is captured in one word—tom. Many translations substitute the word "integrity." In other words, Abimelech is saying, "I took Sarah as my wife in complete integrity—with a clear conscience and clean hands." God knew that, and he spared Abimelech; He kept Abimelech from sinning.

Through the apostle Paul in the New Testament, God has asked us to become individuals of integrity, living our lives with clear consciences and clean hands. Perhaps no area of our lives is more challenging to live with integrity than that of entertainment.

Q&A: *Do you agree that entertainment can sometimes pose a challenge to our integrity? Why or Why not?*

If your conscience has ever worked overtime because of some form of entertainment in which you were engaging, consider yourself blessed. This means you have not become desensitized to what may be inappropriate activities and you are still able to hear the Holy Spirit as He pleads with you to be a man or woman of integrity. It's not that He wants to squelch your fun; He simply wants you to have fun while still honoring Him. This is the kind of fun that allows you to sleep well at night and uphold a credible witness. It allows you to maintain healthy, guilt-free relationships. It permits you to stand before

God and others with a clear conscience and clean hands as an individual of integrity.

Not all "fun" ends in fun. We see this time and again in Scripture, but let's focus on one example. In Exodus 32, we find Moses still up on the mountaintop, speaking with God. He's been there forty days and nights, and the people have grown weary of waiting. The last time they saw Moses, he was entering that volcano, earthquake, thunderstorm phenomenon. For all they knew, he didn't survive, so they sought a new leader in the form of a golden calf and planned a day of celebration and entertainment.

According to Exodus 32:5-6, how did the people entertain themselves?

Does the entertainment appear to be God-honoring?

What did Joshua mistake the partying for in Genesis 32:17?

What did Moses observe as he came near the camp? (Gen 32:19)

It appears that there was a great shortage of clear consciences and clean hands that day. God-honoring worship had been exchanged for "play," and integrity had been traded in for idolatry. Their inappropriate choices ultimately resulted in the death of 3,000 men that day (Ex 32:25-29).

We could get into a great discussion about whether to blame the idolatry for their lapse into poor recreation choices or vice versa, but the fact is the two were connected. God is interested in our entertainment decisions because they can greatly affect our relationship with Him. Good choices can draw us into a closer relationship with Him; bad choices can leave us dancing before a golden calf.

So we would know that it is possible to honor God in our leisure activities, God introduces us to four Hebrew young men in the book of Daniel. The year was 605 B.C., Nebuchadnezzar had defeated the Southern Kingdom, and Daniel, Hananiah, Mishael, and Azariah found themselves among an elite group of young men who were ushered into the king's palace in the entertainment center of the world. Scripture records Daniel's reaction to the new sights and sounds that surrounded him.

According to Daniel 1:8, how does Daniel address the many opportunities set before him?

The other three joined him in his quest to honor God in their food, drink, and recreational activities, and God blessed with incredible health, knowledge, wisdom, and understanding. We soon learn that the young men's resolve would require more than a good, one-time decision. Their desire to honor God would affect every aspect of their lives. The standards they set at the beginning of their immersion into the Babylonian culture would help them make more God-honoring decisions during the tempting years of their captivity.

Like these heroes of faith, we need to resolve not to defile ourselves in our leisure activities. Setting standards before-hand will make it easier for us to recognize and participate in God-honoring entertainment and steer clear of those activities that would lead us away from Him.

As you begin to set entertainment standards, it is important to keep in mind that not all situations will be black and white. The Bible makes some issues extremely clear: "Let us walk properly, as in the day, not in revelry and drunkenness, not in lewdness and lust, not in strife and envy" (Rom 13:13 NIV). There will be some gray issues along the way that you will need to work through, and Paul addresses these gray issues many times in his letters to the churches. He explains his own take on gray issues to the Corinthians in two different chapters.

Read 1 Corinthians 6:12 and 10:23. What important truth does Paul reveal to the believers in Corinth?

He seems to indicate that in gray issues, he is going to err on the side of self-control. This is also the theme of Ephesians 5:3-5 where Paul instructs the church at Ephesus "there must not even be a hint" of sexual immorality or any other activity that is improper for God's holy people. He later admonishes the believers at Thessalonica to "abstain from every form of evil" (1 Thes 5:22). It seems Paul is encouraging all of us to quit asking, "How far can I go?" and instead ask, "How close can I get to God?".

As you work through gray areas, we encourage you to apply the Romans 14 principle. In this chapter, Paul is addressing individuals who believe differently on issues such as eating meat and observing holy days. He's not talking about commandments that are clearly given to all people, such as abstaining from idolatry, adultery, or murder. The issues he is addressing in Chapter 14 seem to allow for more personal direction from God.

According to Romans 14:5, what does Paul say is the key to handling these gray issues?

In our years of working with college students, we have found that many times God will call certain individuals to a higher standard. For instance, the Bible gives some clear guidelines about dating: be equally yoked, flee sexual immorality, edify one another. These apply to all persons. Sometimes, however, God will ask for more. A few years ago, two young girls who came into our lives felt God had asked them to refrain from dating during high school. Another felt God had asked her to save her first kiss until her wedding day. Our own son felt God asking him to fast from dating his first year of college. These are not guidelines that apply to everyone, but Paul would certainly tell these young people, if God lays it on your heart and you are convinced of it, stay true to your convictions.

I (Susan) remember my first real encounter with a conviction in the gray area of dancing. I attended college in the '80s before Student Activity Boards began bringing in bungee jumping and Knockerballs for student recreation. The main event for us was the dance held the first Thursday night of each month. We could barely see one another through the hair spray filled hallways as we made those '80s bangs stand four inches high. Somewhere around the third or fourth month, I began to feel a bit convicted about dolling up and dancing the night away. At first I couldn't put my finger on the reason, but as I prayed it through, I realized my motivation for going to the dances was to build my self-esteem. If guys, cute guys, asked me to dance, my self-esteem soared, but if I found myself drinking more punch and hanging out with the girls, my self-esteem plummeted. God began working in my heart to show me that my identity was to be found in Him alone, not in the number of dance partners who two-stepped my way. I felt Him prodding me to give up this form of entertainment because my motives were not pure.

Not everyone will share this conviction, but what we are asking you to do in the pages that follow is to consider eight popular forms of entertainment and determine how God would have you honor Him through each. Our intentions are not to sway you one way or another but to allow you to seek how God would have you to approach each and then enjoy a meaningful conversation as you discuss them together. Understand that this might require more time and a closer look at Scripture, but knowing where you both stand on these issues will prove extremely beneficial to your relationship. Let's begin.

MUSIC

Henry Wadsworth Longfellow is frequently quoted as saying, "Music is the universal language." Even those of us who can't carry a note in a bucket enjoy cranking up the radio when our favorite tunes come on. We bond with musicians who sing about secret crushes, broken hearts, and pickup trucks.

Q&A: What music do you currently enjoy, and who are some of your favorite musicians?

Do you feel that your music choices are God-honoring? Is there some music that you feel is inappropriate?

What is your plan for honoring God through the entertainment venue of music?

MOVIES/TV SHOWS

The film industry has come a long way from the black and white days of *Leave it to Beaver* and *Abbott and Costello*. Even the Motion Picture Association of America (MPAA) recognized that not all material projected on a screen is suitable for all audiences and developed a film rating scale in 1968. How about you? Have you established a personal rating scale?

Q&A: What movies/TV shows do you currently enjoy? Who are some of your favorite actors/actresses?

Do you feel that your movie/TV show choices are God-honoring?

Are there some movies/TV shows that you feel are inappropriate?

What is your plan for honoring God through the entertainment venue of movies and TV?

BOOKS/ MAGAZINES

I (Susan) have always been a bookworm. While other fifth graders were learning to play sports and musical instruments, I was busy solving mysteries with Nancy Drew and the Hardy

Boys. I still enjoy a good heart-pumping, suspense-filled storyline, but I have had to set some guidelines as to what books and magazines I allow myself to cuddle up with. I found some books led me to have unrealistic expectations of romance and relationships. Others were so well-written that I could easily spend my time helping fictional characters solve their problems rather than investing my life in real people. As a professor of college reading courses, I encourage you to read; as a Christian seeking to honor God, I encourage you to make good choices in what you read.

Q&A: Do you enjoy reading, and if so, what genre do you enjoy most? Do you have a favorite author?

Do you feel that your reading materials are God-honoring?

Are there some reading selections that you feel are inappropriate?

What is your plan for honoring God through the entertainment venue of reading?

DANCING

From proms to Sadie Hawkins nights, schools and organizations have found that dances draw crowds. The majority of those attending do so to make memories and meet new people. Opportunities continue in the adult years with fraternity-sorority dances, community galas, and notorious nightclubs. While dancing was considered a taboo in previous generations, it has made its way into even Christian circles today, often capping off a wedding ceremony or special event. How do you feel about this form of entertainment?

Q&A: *Have you ever attended dances or been a part of the clubbing scene?*

What are your personal views about dancing?

Is there some dancing that is appropriate? Inappropriate?

What is your plan for honoring God through the entertainment venue of dancing?

GAMBLING AND CASINOS

At one time, the mention of gambling conjured up images of dust-covered cowboys sitting around a wooden table in a smoke-filled bar, playing Poker until someone was caught cheating and a brawl broke out. Today, gambling is a multi-billion dollar business with bets being placed on animals, sporting events, and even fantasy teams; Americans spent an estimated $11 million in 2014, betting on teams they owned only in their imagination. Lottery tickets, slot machines, and online gaming have become opportunities to get rich quick.

Q&A: *Is gambling a cause for concern or simply another form of entertainment?*

Have you or do you participate in any form of gambling?

Are there some forms of gambling that you feel are inappropriate?

What is your plan for honoring God through the entertainment venue of gambling?

DRINKING AND DRUGS

Drinking has long been considered a gray issue to many, even in Christian circles. Those who see nothing wrong with it cite verses like 1 Timothy 5:23 where Paul encourages Timothy to "use a little wine for your stomach's sake and your frequent infirmities," and John 2:1-11 where Jesus turns the water into wine. Those who oppose quote verses such as Ephesians 5:18 that states, "Do not be drunk with wine," and Romans 14:21 which declares it good to avoid drinking wine or anything else that will cause a brother to stumble. Not only do you need to give serious consideration to drinking as a form of entertainment, but with the legalization of recreational marijuana becoming more popular, it is also necessary for you to decide where you stand on the use of drugs.

Q&A: What are your personal convictions about drinking?

What are your personal convictions about drugs?

Do you feel that these activities can be God-honoring?

What is your plan for honoring God through the entertainment venues of alcohol and drugs?

SPORTING EVENTS AND VIDEO GAMING

We love competition. Whether we are in the game, physically or virtually, or simply a spectator, we are obsessed with the thrill of declaring a winner. We can drag our lounge chair (complete with cup holders and sunshades) to the nearest field, buy season tickets for our favorite team, or rescue the world from our own recliner. Throw in a hot dog and a bag of pistachio nuts, and life is good. What can you do to make winning calls in this area of entertainment?

Q&A: Do you enjoy sporting events and/or video gaming. If so, what is your favorite?

Do you feel that your sports and video gaming choices are God-honoring?

Are there some sporting events and video games that you feel are inappropriate?

What is your plan for honoring God through the entertainment venue of sports and video gaming?

INTERNET AND SOCIAL MEDIA

According to the 2014 Nielsen's Total Audience Report, Americans spent a little over two hours per day accessing the Internet and social media through Smartphones and PCs.[5] This is nearly 12 percent of our waking hours. The cyber world allures the young and old alike with opportunities to learn new skills, meet new people, and stalk old friends. Can it also be a tool for bringing glory to God?

Q&A: What are the benefits of the Internet and social media?

What are legitimate concerns pertaining to the Internet and social media?

Do you feel that your Internet and social media choices are God-honoring?

What is your plan for honoring God through the entertainment venue of the Internet and social media?

You probably have discovered over the past few pages that setting entertainment standards can be grueling work. We'd like to tell you that the hardest part is behind you, but the truth is, setting standards is only the beginning. Now begins the challenge of living them out, both in your alone time and when you are with others.

We feel it is only fair to caution you that not everyone will share your enthusiasm for making wholesome choices. Like Daniel and his three friends, our standards may set us apart from the crowd and occasionally set us up as targets for ridicule or persecution. Peter eloquently warns of this in 1 Peter 2:11-12.

How does Peter refer to dedicated followers of Christ in these verses?

What does Peter hope that our good choices will ultimately lead to?

It is not always easy to be the "alien and strangers," "sojourners and pilgrims." It can create a downright awkward situation at times. In 1995, we had the opportunity to visit Washington, D.C., to enjoy a conference and a little sightseeing. We were excited about strolling through Smithsonians, photographing monuments, and riding double decker buses. One night had been set aside to go with family and friends to the John F. Kennedy Center for Performing Arts where the theatrical production of the evening was to be *The Bible* in condensed form. Dressed in our best and ready for an inspirational evening, we entered the magnificent building on the Potomac River along with hundreds of other couples and groups. The lights dimmed, the music began, and we sat wide eyed as three men attempted to relay the stories of the Bible in a hurried, humorous, and not-so-accurate manner. We barely made it through a skewed retelling of the story of Adam and Eve before I (Bentley) began to feel extremely uncomfortable. By the time Noah made his appearance on the stage, I had begun silently praying that the rapture would not occur because I did not want to be found in the middle of this production. I knew that I couldn't continue to watch as the Bible and its characters were ridiculed and portrayed as fictional figures without much sense. I told Susan I had to get out immediately. She took my hand, and we made our way up what felt like a thousand stairs. We spent the rest of the night on the back balcony overlooking the river, discussing our desire to honor God in all of our entertainment choices. The standards set that night have sometimes left us feeling a bit like "aliens and strangers," but they have certainly helped us to make better choices over the past two decades.

Q&A: Can you recall a time when you found yourself involved in a form of entertainment where you felt uncomfortable and your conscience was anything but clear?

While entertainment standards may create an occasional awkward moment, they will ultimately set you up for success. The story of Johnny Weissmuller perfectly illustrates this. Johnny was 14 years old when he was discovered by the Illinois Athletic Club swim coach, William Bachrach. Bachrach began an intense training program with the young Johnny, and soon he was clocking an incredible 52 seconds in the 100-yard freestyle. He was unbeatable in his I.A.C. training pool with its dark black striped swimming lanes, but when he competed in unmarked pools at away meets, his performance was less than stellar. Finally, his coach recognized the problem. After losing yet another away meet, Bachrach had Johnny reenter the pool and swim from one end to the other. "Johnny," he exclaimed, "you aren't swimming straight. You don't have that black guide line, and so you are wandering all over the pool." Bachrach then set a hat at the end of the pool and instructed Johnny to draw a mental line to the hat, making it his goal. With an internal straight line connecting Johnny to his goal, his times increased along with his fame. From that point on, Johnny Weissmuller would carry his own "lines" when he went to an unmarked pool, and by staying in those lines, he went on to swim in two Olympic Games and win five Olympic medals. He claimed 52 national championships, broke 67 world records, and won the role as Tarzan in the 1930-40 film series.

The same is true for us. It may be easy to make good decisions concerning entertainment when the lines are clearly drawn, but in those places where the lines aren't clearly marked, we must fix our eyes on the goal and draw an internal line straight to it. Our goal is to know Christ, and the standards we set with His guidance are the internal lines that will make our way straight. It will not be easy, but the reward is Supernatural.

"Let us…fix our eyes on Jesus, the author and finisher of our faith." Hebrews 12:2

Keeping it Real with Nick and Samantha

The dates that are most memorable are not necessarily the ones which cost a lot of money or require a ton of planning; they are the ones that are creative.

Try having a picnic at a lake, state park, nature center or even a national park if one is nearby. Do some hiking, fishing, kayaking, canoeing, or some other outdoor activity that will allow you to explore new territory. Facebook is replete with "best kept secret" places in your state. Take a camera (and a selfie stick) and capture nature's beauty.

Another fun idea is to have an Alphabet Date. Go through the alphabet one letter at a time, creating dates. One night, eat at places and do activities that start with the letter "A", and then move on to other letters. You can plan the date together or surprise one another with an Alphabet date.

It's easy to default to Netflix and popcorn, but memories are made and relationships are built as you enjoy a variety of God-honoring entertainment venues and talk about them for years to come.

Making the Most of Your Meaningful Conversation

1. How did you describe the ideal date at the beginning of the chapter?

2. Which entertainment industry fact surprised you the most?

3. What is one of your favorite entertainment related memories?

4. Do you agree that entertainment can sometimes pose a challenge to your integrity? Why or why not?

5. MUSIC: What music do you currently enjoy, and who are some of your favorite musicians? Do you feel that your music choices are God-honoring? Is there some music that you feel is inappropriate? What is your plan for honoring God through the entertainment venue of music?

6. MOVIES/TV: What movies/TV shows do you currently enjoy? Who are some of your favorite actors/actresses? Do you feel that your movie/TV show choices are God-honoring? Are there some movies/TV shows that you feel are inappropriate? What is your plan for honoring God through the entertainment venue of movies and TV?

7. BOOKS/MAGAZINES: Do you enjoy reading, and if so what genre do you enjoy most? Do you have a favorite author? Do you feel that your reading materials are God-honoring? Are there some reading selections that you feel are inappropriate? What is your plan for honoring God through the entertainment venue of reading?

8. DANCING: Have you ever attended dances or been a part of the clubbing scene? What are your personal views about dancing? Is there some dancing that is appropriate? Inappropriate? What is your plan for honoring God through the entertainment venue of dancing?

9. GAMBLING AND CASINOS: Have you or do you participate in any form of gambling? Are there some forms of gambling that you feel are inappropriate? What is your plan for honoring God through the entertainment venue of gambling?

10. DRINKING AND DRUGS: What are your personal convictions about drinking? What are your personal convictions about drugs? Do you feel that these activities can be God-honoring? What is your plan for honoring God through the entertainment venues of alcohol and drugs?

11. SPORTING EVENTS AND VIDEO GAMING: Do you enjoy sporting events, and if so, what is your favorite? Do you enjoy video gaming? Do you feel that your sports and video gaming choices are God-honoring? Are there some sporting events and video games that you feel are inappropriate? What is your plan for honoring God through the entertainment venue of sports and video gaming?

12. INTERNET AND SOCIAL MEDIA: What are the benefits of the Internet and social media? What are legitimate concerns pertaining to the Internet and social media? Do you feel that your Internet and social media choices are

God-honoring? What is your plan for honoring God through the entertainment venue of the Internet and social media?

13. Can you recall a time when you found yourself involved in a form of entertainment where you felt uncomfortable and your conscience was anything but clear?

14. Spend a few minutes brainstorming fun, God-honoring date ideas.

Chapter 5:

Passion

My conversation becomes quite animated when I talk about
   a) the big game this weekend.
   b) half-price sales.
   c) anything chocolate.
   d) my favorite TV series.

*H*ave you ever had a conversation with a quarterback after Friday night's big game? A recently engaged nineteen-year-old girl? The proud owner of a new car? A deer hunter in the middle of November? It goes without saying there was no shortage of words on their part, and you hardly got a word in edgewise as they relayed details and rattled off plans. You may even have been slightly amused at their facial expressions and body language that communicated you had stumbled upon an important topic in their lives. These conversations are not only entertaining but also indicative of someone who possesses a passion and isn't afraid to share it.

Passions are often easier to recognize than to define. Merriam-Webster takes a stab at defining passion as "a strong feeling or enthusiasm or excitement for something or about doing something." Our college students often describe it as an obsession that can consume a person's thoughts, time, and energy.

Q&A: Who do you know who has an easily recognizable passion? What makes it easy to recognize?

Sometimes passions can begin to show up at an early age. Children become fascinated with an activity and experience a sense of gratification as they receive praise for their efforts. For instance, some children feel empowered with a box of 84 crayons in hand and will fill page after page of a drawing tablet with original masterpieces. Others gravitate toward music, spending hours in front of a mirror, singing into a hairbrush-microphone or practicing dance moves introduced by the latest Disney heartthrob. These childhood interests make for delightful conversations. One of our favorite six-year-olds is currently obsessed with fishing. He will make his way through a crowd to hug our necks and before reaching us is already asking, "The fish in your pond biting this week?" For the next ten minutes, he will enter into a heart-to-heart dialogue about crankbaits and spinners, poppers and plugs. Describe any fish, and he can tell you what it is and where it can be caught, and his best friend is *The Fishing Channel*. Whether he grows up to be the next Ernest Hemingway or Jimmy Houston, one thing is for certain—he has a childhood passion for fishing.

Q&A: Did you have any childhood interests or passions?

During the teen years, passions often take on the shape of hobbies or favorite pastimes. School introduces new experiences in sports, the arts, or organizational leadership. Although dreams of fame and fortune still consume our thoughts, we begin to think a bit more realistically and focus our time and efforts on activities in which we seem to excel. A high school freshman may spend hours in the gym perfecting a three-point shot to make the varsity team. Music lovers find an empty basement or garage for jam sessions on their way to stardom. These are the years that cliques emerge, most of them being based on shared passions.

Q&A: What clique did you find yourself running in during your teen years? Did you share a common passion? If not, what was your passion during these years?

While some passions may slip into the category of hobbies and favorite pastimes, others will become deciding factors in career choices. Not ready to let go of his passion for the sport of soccer, a young man may pursue a degree in education and coaching. The Valedictorian with a passion for history trivia may seek employment as a museum docent. The auto aficionado may turn that passion into a full-time career in vehicle maintenance.

Q&A: Based on your interests or passions, what would be your dream job?

We've discussed passions that serve as interests, hobbies, and even careers, but there is another kind of passion that many of us will encounter over the course of our lives. This is a God-given passion that often hits us out of nowhere as we are simply doing life. It can still create excitement and consume our thoughts, time, and energy, but it usually finds its origin in a relationship with God. In his book, *What You Do Best in the Body of Christ*, Author Bruce Bugbee defines this kind of passion as "the God-given desire of the heart to make a kingdom difference somewhere." And this seems to be a kind of passion that God incites and commends in Scripture.

Q&A: Can you think of any individuals in the Bible who possessed a God-given passion?

Immediately, we think of David. True, sometimes his passions got him in trouble, but those that were God-given certainly set him apart as one of the godliest leaders in Israel's history. He had a passion for worship, and we see this in the music he played, the way he danced, the words he wrote, and the temple he longed to build. He speaks of this passion for worship in Psalm 69:9 when he writes, "Zeal for your house has eaten me up." It was more than a passion for a building; it was a passion for the worship of God that would take place within it.

Another passionate Bible character that comes to mind is Nehemiah. When he heard about the broken wall of Jerusalem, he sat down and wept, mourned, fasted, and prayed. During this time, God placed a passion for the rebuilding of the wall in Nehemiah's heart, and he determined to make a difference in the homeland of his fathers. He was consumed with the task and driven by his desire to see God glorified in the holy city. The result was a wall that was built in a remarkable 52 days and still stands today.

Lest we begin to think only men can possess God-ordained passion, turn to Acts 9:36 and read through the remainder of the chapter.

According to these verses, what was Tabitha's (aka Dorcas) passion?

This woman combined her passion for widows and the poor with her ability to sew; as a result, many people believed in the Lord.

God-given passions did not die with the first-century believers. He continues to place desires in the hearts of His followers today. These passions often revolve around a problem or cause, such as abuse, depression, disease or social issues. We recently heard of a young woman who would drive through the streets in China, praying for the city. As she did, God stirred her heart about the brothels and prostitutes that lined the streets. She took up the cause of delivering scones and the Good News to these red light districts. Then God impressed upon her the need these women would have for a new job when they accepted Christ and the more abundant life He offers. Never having run a business before, she opened a bakery and a door for young women desperate for a new start.[6]

Q&A: Are there any problems, causes, or social issues that seem to draw your attention? (Abortion, AIDS, human trafficking, persecution, etc.)

Passions can also focus on a particular people group, such as children, young couples, the elderly, and the family. Before Susan and I ever started dating, God placed a passion in our hearts for college students and young adults. Imagine our surprise when we learned that we shared not only an attraction for one another but a common passion. Two months after our wedding, we boarded a plane and headed to Hawaii to serve as semester missionaries and start Bible studies on three community college campuses. God confirmed our call, and we returned to the mainland to pursue the Master's degrees that would allow us to invest our lives in this age group. Nearly three decades later, the passion for this age group is still strong. It seems almost unfair to accept a salary for something we enjoy doing so much.

Q&A: Is there a particular age group or people group toward whom you find yourself gravitating? (Children, teens, young adults, expectant mothers, etc.)

Sometimes a passion is directly related to ministry, such as music, youth, preaching, prayer, or missions. William came to Oklahoma from the country of Rwanda as a twenty-year-old Pre-Engineering major. He immediately won our hearts with his humble ways and ready smile. After a few minutes into any conversation, it became obvious this young man was wise beyond his years, and it was no wonder—William had a passion for prayer. In those hours together, William learned things about God and from God. During praise and worship services, William would often turn to face the wall where he could become completely focused on the praises and prayers he would lift to heaven. He took seriously Jesus's admonition to observe fasting and did so in a quiet way that never drew attention to himself. When called upon to pray in public, William would begin a respectful yet comfortable dialogue with God that often became a worship service itself. And God used his passion for prayer as an instrument of blessing to everyone around him. On several occasions, William came to us in tears, amazed at how God had met needs he had never shared with anyone but God. While William had many talents and gifts, his passion was for prayer.

Q&A: Have you felt a calling or passion toward a particular area of ministry? (Children's ministry, youth ministry, collegiate ministry, video, bus, preaching, missions, etc.)

A biblical study of passions reveals there is no formula or guidelines, no set way of receiving or using, a God-given desire. Some seem to last a lifetime; others are for a season. What does appear to be consistent is the purpose of these passions.

Read Romans 12:10-11. What are we to do with our "zeal" and "spiritual fervor"?

These passions are to be used to love others and serve the Lord. Passions are not opportunities to seek self-glory and gain attention and approval. They were never meant to become a personal agenda but a platform for God's glory. The Greek word for glory is *Doxa,* and it means to make God recognizable. That's what our passions are to do—make God recognizable. We see this in 20th-century heroes of the faith.

Corrie ten Boom and her family had a passion for the Jewish community during Hitler's reign of terror. They were consumed with the desire to make a difference where they were and how they could. Their passion drove them to risk their lives to provide refuge to complete strangers. It was a costly passion, but through the testimony and actions of this family, God was and continues to be made recognizable.

The same is true of the life of Jim Elliott. God planted a passion for unreached people groups in Jim's heart while he was a student at Wheaton College. Immediately he began preparing himself for wherever God might lead. He would try any kind of food to develop a pallet for even the most unappetizing dishes. He exercised regularly, not to boast of guns and packs, but to discipline his body for whatever adventure God might set before him. The passion to take the gospel to those who had never heard eventually led him to the Wadoni tribe in Ecuador. Many would say that same passion cost him his life as Elliott and four others were massacred by the Wadoni tribe, but not before the gospel was shared, and Elliott's team made God recognizable to their very assassins. Because of Jim's zeal and spiritual fervor, many Acuas became believers. Even decades after his death, Jim Elliott continues to make God recognizable to all who read his story.

In both of these examples, we find individuals who first of all loved the Lord and were serving Him faithfully. He then placed a passion in their hearts and invited them to be co-laborers in His specific work at a specific time. This seems to be how most God-given passions are birthed. That's why it is difficult for us to muster up a passion on our own. We don't have the luxury of scrolling through current events and picking the issue for which we want to become passionate. Kingdom-focused passions are purpose-filled treasures from God. Understanding this first of all, is there anything we can do to prepare for and recognize a heaven-given passion? Even though there is no formula for discovering a passion, there does seem to be some wise, biblical advice for preparing to receive one.

Passion Preparation

1. Explore More.

Place yourself in situations where God can enlighten the eyes of your heart (Ephesians 1:18) to the people and situations around you. Attend conferences, take classes, and get training that will help you to grow in your personal walk with Christ. Volunteer for worthwhile projects even if it pushes you out of your comfort zone. Find legitimate organizations and learn what they are doing to advance the gospel. Even if none of these immediately unveil a deep-seated passion, they will endow you with a more biblical, others-centered, global worldview.

2. Exercise gifts.

At the moment of salvation, believers receive from the Holy Spirit at least one spiritual gift for "equipping the saints for the work of the ministry for the edifying of the body of Christ" (Ephesians 4:12). You may have heard it said that God equips those He calls, and this is especially true where passions are concerned. Many times our passions provide opportunities to use our spiritual gifts. For this reason, it may be well worth your time to read through the lists of spiritual gifts located in Romans 12, 1 Corinthians 12, and Ephesians 4. You can also take an online spiritual gift inventory on a credible website. Since it is often easier to identify spiritual gifts in others than in ourselves, it may be beneficial to seek wise counsel from another believer concerning your spiritual gift. Once you are familiar with what your spiritual gift is, be sure to seek ways to use it and allow God to develop it.

Q&A: What do you feel may be a spiritual gift God has given to you?

3. Edify others.

Keep in mind that spiritual gifts and God-given passions are always given to glorify God and edify others. Purpose each day to look beyond yourself and "look out for the interests of others" (Phil 2:4). Many times it is in serving others that a passion develops.

Passion Cautions

Just as the Bible provided insightful advice in preparing to receive a passion, it also gives several cautions about receiving one.

1. Make sure your passion is good.

Take a close look at Galatians 4:18. When does Paul say it is good to be zealous?

Paul was qualified to speak to us on this one because he had certainly been zealous for a bad purpose—the abolishing of Christianity. Paul encourages us to learn from his mistake and realize that God-given passions will always be consistent with the Word, promote obedience, and glorify God, not self.

2. Understand your passion is given by God to YOU.

Many times we have students come to us, passionately sharing what God is laying on their heart, but they conclude their eloquent presentation by asking us to do something about it. We used to feel it was our responsibility to do something with every passion and plea brought before us, but over time we have learned that God usually gives the passion to the one He is calling to do something. Don't expect others to see your passion through; remember that if He has given you the passion, He will also equip you to see it through. Along these same lines, it's important to realize not everyone will share your enthusiasm. Jeremiah had been given a passion to preach God's Word, describing it as "a burning fire shut up in my bones" he could not hold back (20:9). In Jeremiah 18-19, we find him using a potter's flask to proclaim passionately God's exact words. The chief governor and priest, Pashur, didn't share Jeremiah's passion for truth and sentenced him to a beating and the stocks. In Psalm 69:8-12, David explains that his "zeal for the house" of the Lord has made him a stranger to his own family. From these and other examples, we learn that not everyone will share our passion, which leads us to the last caution.

3. Realize pursuing a passion may not be convenient or easy.

It wasn't for Jeremiah, David, or Paul; Jim Elliott, Corrie ten Boom, or Christ Himself. However, each of these would testify that pursuing their God-given passion was worth whatever sacrifice it required. They have set incredible examples for us of choosing holy over easy and are now reaping eternal benefits. Pursuing our passions won't always be easy. It may cost us emotionally, physically, relationally, even financially, but in the words of Beth Moore, "the trade-off is a spin around Planet Earth that actually means something. I am convinced that when the last chapter of each life story is recorded in the annals of heaven, people would rather have lived out their fullness of days with purpose than without pain" (*Looking Up when Life is Looking Down*).

Where does the passionate, purpose-filled life begin? It must begin with a growing relationship with Jesus Christ. Our greatest passion should always remain the one expressed by Paul in Philippians 3:7-10: I count all things loss...that I may know Him.

Q&A: Has God given you a passion for anything at this point in your life, and if so, what are you doing about it?

Keeping it Real with Nick and Samantha

If you're continually looking for creative date ideas, why not try planning dates around a specific cause or act of service? For instance,

- Around Valentine's Day, buy a box of Valentine cards and hand them out at a local nursing home.
- Run (or walk) together in a cancer awareness, Cystic Fibrosis, or any specific cause event.
- Volunteer at a children's home or as mentors for an after school program.
- Spend a Saturday caring for an elderly person's yard.
- Volunteer to babysit for a young couple for a few hours so that they can enjoy a dinner together.

Galatians 6:10 urges us to do good to all people when we have the opportunity. Why not allow your dates to become those opportunities and enjoy time with one another while doing good for others?

Making the Most of Your Meaningful Conversation

1. How did you answer the animated conversations question at the beginning of the chapter? What merits your most animated conversations?

2. Who do you know that has an easily recognizable passion? What makes it easy to recognize?

3. Did you have any childhood interests or passions?

4. What clique did you find yourself running in during your teen years? Did you share a common passion? If not, what was your passion during these years?

5. Based on your interests or passions, what would be your dream job?

6. Which individuals in the Bible came to mind when you thought of those with a God-given passion?

7. Are there any problems, causes, or social issues that seem to draw your attention?

8. Is there a particular age group or people group toward whom you find yourself gravitating?

9. Have you felt a calling or passion toward a particular area of ministry?

10. What do you feel may be a spiritual gift God has given to you?

11. Has God given you a passion for anything at this point in your life, and if so, what are you doing about it?

12. Spend a few minutes planning a date night that would involve serving someone else.

Chapter 6:

Church

My earliest memories of church involve
   a) a costumed role in a Christmas play.
   b) groovin' to Vacation Bible School music.
   c) eating play dough in the Toddler's room.
   d) sleepless nights at church camp.
   e) other: _____

Whether you grew up in church or not, chances are you have some early recollection of a church experience. Maybe it was nervously reciting Bible verses to earn candy or badges, riding on a church bus, or watching a friend be baptized.

I (Bentley) remember smells. When I was a child, we met in an old two-room schoolhouse that had been converted into a church, and I can still smell the gas stove that was used to heat it. I also remember the smell of fruit on the Sunday morning before Christmas when all the kids were given sacks with apples, oranges, and nuts. I recall events like making trips to the outhouse (yes, they still existed in the sixties), having thumb wars on the back pew, and scaring a nursery worker when she was coming down a dark hall by hiding and growling when she got near. I remember playing Crack the Whip with the other kids and the trip to the hospital that followed when my sister got her whip cracked and broke her collarbone. I also remember people like the music minister who would let my brother help him direct the songs, Miss Madge who made a strawberry cake for every church social, and the man who prayed "Our Dear Heavenly Father" in the deepest voice I had ever heard. A good number of my childhood memories center around the small churches where I grew up.

Q&A: What about you? What are some of your earliest church memories?

When we are younger, the church often represents a place where we can go to be with friends, learn about God, and possibly fall in love. Much of the reason we attend is to be with others or to keep our parents happy. The church serves as a safe place for social gatherings and Christian encouragement. But as we grow, so does our understanding of the church.

Q&A: As you have gotten older, how has your idea of church changed?

I'm reminded of a line from the movie *Prince Caspian* from the *Chronicles of Narnia* series. Lucy is reunited with Aslan, and looking into his face, she says, "You seem bigger." Aslan wisely replies, "Every year you grow, you find me bigger." This is true of our understanding of God. As we grow spiritually, we find Him to be bigger than we ever imagined. As we grow spiritually, we also find the concept of church and the role it plays in our relationship with God is much bigger than we had first imagined. Church becomes a great deal more than a building with a steeple, a fellowship with food, or a youth group with hot girls. It becomes a body of believers with a mission and a purpose.

Q&A: How would you describe the mission/ purpose of the church? Based on the mission you described, how do you feel the church as a whole is doing? Are we moving in a positive direction?

Over the past 2000 years, the church has certainly faced its share of problems. The Lord never promised that the church would be a safe zone, free from challenges and objections. In fact, Christ seems to suggest the opposite— He warns His disciples that there will be false teachers, deceptive doctrines, political pressures, and ruthless persecution. Despite efforts to crush, silence, and exterminate the church, it still stands and will continue to stand as a testimony of Christ's power.

Q&A: What do you feel may be the greatest challenges facing the church today?

Many people have become frustrated or disillusioned with the church today. Some refer to it as an organized religion and have stopped going altogether. In fact, 30% of American says they seldom or never attend church. Only 20-40% report attending church on a regular basis. That leaves 30-50%, or as many as half, as infrequent attenders.[7] The percentage of weekly attenders has slightly decreased in the last decade while the number of non-attenders has slightly increased. What reasons have you heard for not attending and being an active part of a local body of believers?

We work with young adults, aged 18-25. This age group reportedly has the greatest number of church "drop outs." Reasons cited often revolve around life changes such as moving away to college, working on Sundays, or change in friends, but we hear four reasons repeatedly.

Q&A: How might you respond to the following reasons for "quitting church"?

Reasons for Not Attending Church

1.   The church is full of hypocrites.

Perhaps this is the one we hear most frequently, and we always agree. The word for *hypocrite* comes from a Greek term commonly used of actors on the Greek stage, and every church is certain to have a few actors. Jesus predicted this in Matthew 13:24-30 through the parable of the wheat and tares. But every church is also certain to have believers who are genuinely seeking to love God and to love others. It seems unfair to judge an entire church by a few members who may be making bad decisions.

2.   I've been hurt by the church.

Because the church is comprised of imperfect people, relationship issues are bound to occur. Sometimes hurtful words are exchanged, and inappropriate actions are taken. As many reading this have experienced first-hand, no pain is greater than that afflicted by a brother or sister; however, withdrawing from the church is not the answer. A few years ago, we were visiting with an elderly woman who had dropped out of church at the age of fifteen. A couple of deacons had approached her about her clothing, and she was offended. To punish them and God, she vowed to never attend church again. We apologized for the comments those deacons had made years ago, but the truth is her withdrawal from church didn't hurt anyone but herself. She wasn't punishing those deacons. She wasn't even punishing God. She was punishing herself, refusing to be a part of a good plan that God had for her life.

3.   I don't get anything out of church.

Most of us have sat through a service or two and felt like our time would have been better spent flying a kite, but that doesn't mean we quit going.

I (Bentley) love to eat. I especially enjoy a big, juicy steak. As much as I enjoy steaks, I realize that not every meal can be steak, and I certainly didn't acquire this 300-pound figure by refusing to eat anything but steak. It's the same way spiritually. We can't expect every message to be a Sermon on the Mount or bring down tongues of fire like the preaching at Pentecost. Some messages are going to hit closer to where we live than others, but God has made a couple of promises we probably need to remember before making the statement that we "don't get anything out of church." First of all, He assures us in Isaiah 55:11 that His Word will not return void. It is as powerful as a two-edged sword, and it will accomplish what He pleases. Secondly, Hebrews 11:6 tells us that God rewards those who earnestly seek Him. If I don't get anything out of church, perhaps it is because I haven't come seeking. I've taken this seriously the last few years and have found when I go to church anticipating a word from God, seeking it earnestly, He always provides.

4. I don't have to go to church to be a Christian.

True. We are saved by grace, through faith, "not of works lest anyone should boast" (Eph 2:8-9). But if we are Christians, we will want to obey Christ and follow His example, and where was He every Sabbath? According to Luke 4:16, Jesus went to Nazareth where "as His custom was, He went into the synagogue on the Sabbath day." A few verses later in Luke 4:31, we find Him in Capernaum where He "was teaching them on the Sabbaths" in the synagogue. Two chapters later in Luke 6:6, "He entered the synagogue and taught" on another Sabbath. Three times within three chapters we are reminded that if it was the Sabbath, Jesus was in the synagogue. It makes sense that, as His followers, the church is where we should be on our day of worship, too.

This last explanation renders invalid any reason a believer can give for not attending church. If anyone knew there were hypocrites in the church, it was Jesus, and yet where could He be found every Sabbath? If anyone had experienced hurt from the church, it was Jesus, yet where did He return every

Sabbath? If anyone could have found a sermon preached by mere men less than exciting, it was Jesus. After all, it would be impossible to preach a story or Scripture with which He wasn't already familiar. And yet He trusted His Father to make the most of those moments in the synagogue. Finally, if anyone didn't have to go to church to have a relationship with God, it was Jesus. He was one with the Father already, yet He "humbled Himself and become obedient" to keep the Sabbath holy, even to the point of death (Phil 2:8). Why do we continue to associate with the church and all its flaws? Because Jesus did. Even with all its quirks and imperfections, Jesus loved the church and gave His life for her (Eph 5:25).

Every year we meet young people who profess they love the Lord, some of them even surrendering to missions or other ministries, but these same individuals have become disenchanted with the church and rarely attend. They say they love Jesus, just not the church.

Q&A: *Is it possible to love Jesus but not the church?*

When Susan and I began dating, I could hardly wait to introduce her to my family. I loved her, and I desperately wanted my family to love her, too. Fortunately they did, and twenty-seven years later, we are still enjoying the benefits of a close-knit family. But what if my family had decided not to accept Susan? What if they had said, "Bentley, we love you, but we don't approve of your choice of a bride. We want to have a relationship with you but not her." Well, you can see where things could get complicated. We planned to be a package deal. Jesus calls the church His bride, and it brings Him great delight when we choose to love the church. His desire is that as we fall in love with Him, we would also fall in love with His bride. The two are a package deal.

Q&A: *How do you feel you are doing in the area of loving the church?*

As we fall more in love with Christ and His church, we will quit complaining about what the church is not and begin to see it for what it could be. We will find passages like Acts 2:40-47 to be both challenging and exciting and will begin to pray and long for the church described in these verses.

Q&A: What parts of the description in Acts 2 do you feel constitute a good church?

These new believers were enjoying a unique fellowship, but they fully understood that their main purpose for existing was to honor God with their lives. They were not the charter chapter of a social organization or community center for public events. They were much more. Social clubs and community centers enrich lives and have their place, but the church with Christ as its foundation would deal with issues of eternal life and death. For this reason, the early disciples spent much time studying the teachings of Christ and continuing "steadfastly in the apostles' doctrines" (Acts 2:42). They wanted to make sure truth was being taught, and they committed themselves to seeking diligently for that truth, both corporately and privately.

Even today, the primary characteristic of a healthy church is the clear, uncompromising preaching and teaching of God's Word. This must include the truth that Jesus is "the way, the truth, and the life; no man comes to the Father" except through Him (John 14:6). In Matthew 16, Christ asks His disciples whom they believe Him to be. Peter replies, "You are the Christ, the Son of the living God." Jesus commends his answer and declares that upon this truth the church will be built. Two thousand years later, this is still the foundational truth that distinguishes the church from all other collective groups.

With faith in Christ and commitment to God's Word as its foundation, the early church then moved forward to seek God's will in other related matters. The book of Acts is a record of their discussions and conclusions, many of which were recorded by the Council of Nicea in 325 A.D. While Christians today continue to agree on the divinity of Christ and the relationship we can now have with God because of Jesus's life, death, and resurrection, differing views on some issues of theology have resulted in a plethora of denominations. As you mature in Christ, it is important to know what you believe and why you believe it where these doctrinal issues are concerned.

Q&A: This may be a good time to discuss some key doctrinal issues.
What do you believe Scripture teaches about church practices and ordinances, such as baptism, the Lord's Supper, tithing, the biblical definition of the family, evangelism, the Sabbath, end times, and other issues you deem important?

This early New Testament body of believers became the paradigm for the church through which God delights to work. They were experiencing life to the fullest by living out the greatest commandments of loving God and loving others. It is as if this group enjoyed being with one another and couldn't limit church to just one day. This surely made the Father smile because His plan for the church has always been so much more than a couple of services each week.

Jesus viewed His relationship with the church as a covenant and describes it as such in Ephesians 5. Often this chapter is used as an admonition to husbands and wives, but in 5:32, Paul explains that he is actually talking about the relationship between Christ and the church. Think about it this way. When you see a shadow, is it the real thing? Of course not, it is an outline, a vague image of that which is real. In Ephesians 5, Paul explains that a marriage between a man and a woman is a shadow; the real covenant is between Christ and the church. Sometimes we get so hung up on "submit to your own husbands" and "love your wives" that we miss Paul's main point. For thirteen verses, he works diligently to reveal that the purpose of a Christian marriage is to cause those around us to look to the real covenant relationship that exists between Christ and His church. Earthly marriage is a shadow of the ultimate covenant between Christ and the church.

When we begin to think of our involvement in a church as a covenant, it takes on new meaning. Suddenly it is more than an option, a past time, or a responsibility. It is a relationship, and like all other relationships, it can only grow and flourish with time, attention, and commitment of all parties involved. Just as a couple will exchange vows, pledging themselves to one another as they enter into a marriage covenant, believers pledge themselves to one another and to Christ and enter into a church covenant. God has not left us to guess at what this covenant is to look like; Scripture is replete with examples and instructions for how to live in this covenant community.

The Church as a Covenant Community

1. We covenant to love one another.

A few years ago, our church was going through a difficult time when I (Susan) divinely stumbled upon Romans 12:10. Speaking to the church at Rome, Paul exhorts the believers to "be devoted to one another in love. Honor one another above yourselves" (NIV).

It was as if the word "devoted" leaped off the page at me. I liked these people I called my church family. I was interested in them and their well-being, but *devoted* seemed to be asking for a bit more. For instance, a devoted husband is someone who is loyal to his family, making sacrifices for their well-being and doing whatever it takes to demonstrate his love for them. That seems a little different than being willing to share a pew. Being devoted seems to carry the connotation we are in this thing together, come what may. That I will make time to pray for them, listen to them, truly love them, even when it is not convenient or easy.

Q&A: What does the word devoted mean to you? What would it look like to be "devoted to one another in love" within the church?

It is not uncommon to find young people who are attending three different churches during any given week. You have to applaud their desire to meet with other believers; however, it's hard to be devoted while running in different directions. Perhaps a better plan is to find a Bible-teaching church and be devoted, faithful, and loyal, learning what it means to enjoy a covenant community.

Devoted also seems to indicate a sense of permanence. This is a revolutionary idea in a day when Christians are notorious for changing churches as frequently as we do our clothes. During that difficult season at our church, it was tempting to move on to another church that seemed to be growing and thriving, but God continued to burn Romans 12:10 into our hearts. We searched through Scripture trying to find something that would support a church hop, but instead what we found were are only two reasons for breaking the covenant relationship with our local church: false teachings or because God makes it clear that He intends to use us somewhere else.

Personality issues do not appear to be a justifiable reason to change churches. Paul makes this clear in the way he addresses two women, Euodia and Syntyche, who seem to be having a difference of opinion in the Philippian church (4:1-7). He urges them to work it out because God is made recognizable when we go against human nature and choose His nature instead. One of the last things Christ prayed for during His final hours on earth was for the unity of believers evidenced in our devotion to God and one another (John 17:11, 20-23).

Q&A: When do you consider it permissible to change from one church to another?

2. We covenant to serve together.

As we discussed in the last chapter, God gives every believer a spiritual gift of His choosing to use in the building up and edification of the church. This gift is not to draw attention to self but is for the express purpose of serving those to whom we are devoted. In three different letters—Romans, 1 Corinthians, and Ephesians—Paul reminds us that if we are not using our spiritual gift within the church, we are causing the church to be weaker. Not only are we weakening the church, but we are stunting our own spiritual growth. There is something about serving others that gives our lives purpose. We become more like Jesus when we take up the towel and basin and kneel to wash the feet of others through acts of service.

We serve one another because we realize that by doing so, we ultimately serve God. Take a minute to read 1 Peter 4:10-11. According to the last words of verse 11, why do we serve?

Q&A: Have you found a place to serve others in your local church? If, so, where?

3. *We covenant to worship together.*

We often talk of "worship services," leading "worship," and "praise and worship teams," making the word *worship* a difficult one to define. Our understanding of it comes from the Old English word which means "worth-ship," or the idea of ascribing worth to someone or something. The Bible is filled with the testimonies of people who worshiped the Lord, the first being Abraham in Genesis 22. Abraham declared his mission on Mount Moriah to be one of worship (22:4), and certainly it was as he climbed those rocks with Isaac that day to reveal God's "worth" in his life. In an incredible act of provision, God explains the test and allows Abraham to witness first-hand how magnificent He is. This was not a moment Abraham could create on his own; true worship rarely is. Rather, worship can be defined as catching a glimpse of who God is, which then leads us to ascribe proper worth to Him.

Think of Isaiah, surrounded by burning coals and singing seraphim. At that moment, Isaiah caught a glimpse of who God is, and the result was genuine worship. Think of the disciples who watched from the side of a rocking boat as Jesus walked on water and rescued a sinking Peter. At that moment, they caught a glimpse of who Jesus really is, and Matthew 14:33 records their responses as they "worshiped Him, saying 'Truly You are the Son of God.'" Think of any great worship service or moment in Scripture, and you will find it is the result of an individual or group catching a glimpse of who God is, and the result is genuine worship.

As a church, it becomes our desire to catch a glimpse of who God is and our responsibility to invite Him to make Himself recognizable. Sometimes He does this through a song, a sermon, a service project, a testimony, or even a trial. He can provide these glimpses anytime and anywhere He chooses. While it is true we can worship God by ourselves, how exciting it is when He allows us to experience these glimpses with fellow believers, inviting us to be a part of corporate worship and a miracle moment.

Q&A: Can you recall a time when you caught a glimpse of who God is and the result was genuine worship?

4. We covenant to do life together.

This seems to be the picture of the New Testament church in Acts 2:42-47. Reread this passage. If you were making a movie about Acts 2, how would this scene look?

Acts 2:44 reveals "all who believed were together, and had all things in common." Under the common banner of Christ and with the common goal of glorifying Him, these believers were eating together, studying together, praising God together, witnessing to others together, even solving financial dilemmas together. The result was beautiful as "the Lord added to the church daily those who were being saved" (Acts 2:47).

Then and now, God has great plans for the church. Sometimes we forget that the church was His idea. It was not invented by man, and it will not survive by the hands of man. It is His chosen tool for growing the saints and reaching the world. The church is a gift from God to His children. Granted, sometimes it feels more like a curse. He never said it would be easy to be devoted to this mosaic of imperfect people. But still, He declares it necessary.

Like any gift, we enjoy it more when we understand its purpose. When our nephew Jake was six, we bought him a small telescope for Christmas. He ripped off the red and green paper and waved the telescope in the air, yelling, "I love it! It's just what I've always wanted!" Then he brought it down to eye level for a closer look, puckered his lips, and asked, "What is it?" Perhaps the church is that kind of gift. Out of our love for the Giver, we at first exclaim, "I love it; it's just what I've always wanted," but upon a closer look, we turn to God and ask, "What is it?"

Just like we did for Jake that Christmas many years ago, God smiles and patiently explains the purpose of His gift to those who want to know. He reminds us to be realistic in our expectations. The church is not perfect; it's a work in progress. But it is under the direction of Christ Himself, and we can be confident that "He who has begun a good work in you will complete it" (Phil 1:6). He is very much involved, growing and perfecting the church so that He might present her to Himself as a glorious, blemish-free bride someday (Eph 5:27). Christ hasn't given up on the Church, and we can't either.

A few months ago, we broke our College/Career Sunday school class into small groups and asked them to draw a picture of what they think of when they hear the word *church*. They created pictures of Bibles, stained glass, a dove in flight, a building with a steeple, and a field full of lambs. The one that really caught our attention was of a conveyor belt with people sitting on it. It depicted the idea of church as a place where we go through the motions with others who are doing the same. Perhaps that was your idea of church ten pages ago. If so, we pray God has shown you that His plan for the church is so much more. Keep asking Him to show you what His plan for the church is, and celebrate the covenant community of which He has invited you to be a part as you learn that church is not someplace to go—it is a family where you belong.

Q&A: When you hear the word church now, what image comes to mind? Attempt to draw that image in the space below.

Q&A: At the beginning of this chapter, we remembered your church-past. We then discussed your church-present. What would you like your church-future to be?

Keeping it Real with Nick and Samantha

In Matthew 20:28, Jesus said that He had not come to be served but to serve. As Christians, we shouldn't think of church as a place for us to be served. We must model ourselves after Christ and become servants by joining with our brothers and sisters in Christ and reaching out to others. God has given each of us talents and abilities; it is our responsibility to use them for His glory and to do our part in being His hands and feet.

For a dating couple, it is often difficult to decide where to go to church. When we began dating, we were both active members of different churches in the same town. After praying about this carefully, we felt it would be best to stay where we were and continue serving rather than going to one church together all the time. Occasionally, we would attend services at each other's church so that we could get to know the important people in each other's life, but for the most part, God led us to stay in our own churches and continue to worship and serve until our vows were exchanged.

Whether you attend church together or separately, encourage one another to make the time to go and grow with a local body of believers. It is an important part of honoring God and maintaining a God-honoring relationship.

Making the Most of Your Meaningful Conversation

1. How did you answer the multiple-choice question about your earliest church memories at the beginning of the chapter? Share some of your earliest church memories with each other, including sights, sounds, smells, people, and events.

2. As you've gotten older, how has your idea of church changed?

3. How would you describe the mission/ purpose of the church? Based on the mission you described, how do you feel the church as a whole is doing? Are we moving in a positive direction?

4. What do you feel may be the greatest challenges facing the church today?

5. Of the reasons discussed for not attending church, which one have you heard most often and how do you respond to that reason?

6. Do you feel it is possible to love Jesus but not the church?

7. How do you feel you are doing in the area of loving the church?

8. What parts of the description in Acts 2 do you feel constitute a good church?

9. Spend a little time discussing key doctrinal issues, such as what you believe Scripture teaches about baptism, the Lord's Supper, tithing, the biblical definition of the family, evangelism, the Sabbath, end times, and other issues you deem important.

10. What does the word *devoted* mean to you? What would it look like to be "devoted to one another in love" within the church?

11. When do you consider it permissible to change from one church to another?

12. Have you found a place to serve others in your local church? If so, where?

13. Can you recall a time when you caught a glimpse of who God is and the result was genuine worship?

14. Share and explain your drawing of church.

15. What would you like your church-future to be?

Chapter 7:

Family

Which popular TV/movie family best depicts your own and why?
- a) The Cleavers (*Leave it to Beaver*)
- b) The Robertsons (*Duck Dynasty*)
- c) The Addams (*Addams Family*)
- d) The Parrs (*The Incredibles*)
- e) other: _____

*O*ne of our favorite activities as a family has always been playing games. Yahtzee, Uno, Skipbo, Chicken Foot, you name it, we love to play it. Except Monopoly. Monopoly is not a game; it's a Medieval torture device packaged in an attractive box. Other than that game that never ends, we have always loved pulling chairs around a circle table and unleashing our competitive spirits. When our children were young, we had just finished a round of Spoons in which our six-year-old son missed out on a spoon. He made a face we had never seen him make before. His eyes and mouth were open as wide as they could get, then he curled his top lip under and slid it up over his teeth onto his gums. Our daughter immediately declared he looked like a beaver, and we began to laugh hysterically because he did. One by one, we each made the beaver face until someone yelled out "One, Two, Three, Four, let's all do the beaver roar," after which we all made the face and growled with our "paws" in the air. We bent over in our chairs, laughing until tears streamed down our faces. Suddenly, our son, with a puzzled and somewhat fearful look on his face, stopped laughing and asked, "Hey, are we normal?"

While we still laugh about that moment so many years ago, I (Susan) have to admit that I've asked that question about our family many times over the years. If you're honest, you probably have, too. Whether you come from a family as wholesome as the Cleavers or as dysfunctional as Homer Simpson's, there have probably been times when you wondered about the normalcy of those you have been assigned to do life with.

Q&A: Have you ever wondered whether your family is normal? Can you remember a time in the past or recently when this question came to mind? What are some of the quirks and idiosyncrasies that show up in your family?

In 2003, John Ortberg came out with a new book entitled, *Everybody's Normal...until you get to know them.* While the content of the book is excellent, it is the title itself that I have quoted and taken great solace in over the years. Every family looks normal from a distance, even ours. But as you get to know the individuals that make up that family, you learn every family has its quirks, idiosyncrasies, and beaver moments. Not even the Cleavers were normal. I mean, who honestly vacuums their home in high heels and pearls? The truth is, every family is dysfunctional to some degree or another. For some, this may be embarrassing, but for most of us, this is freeing. Our family isn't perfect—big deal. Neither is anyone else's. We would all agree there has only been one perfect person to walk the face of the earth, and it wasn't any of us. Since a family is made up of imperfect individuals, it stands to reason there is no perfect family

When we give up on the idea of being a part of a perfect family and begin to embrace the idea we are instead a part of an imperfectly normal family, we can start to appreciate and even enjoy one another. While a group of people may share a name or bloodline, it can still be comprised of very different personalities. This is not a bad thing. A great team always boasts of diversity. Take for instance a basketball team. If everyone was 6'7" and determined to play the post, what kind of madness would ensue in those few feet inside the paint? What NBA team boasts of five point guards on the floor at the same time? The strength of a basketball team lies in the individuality of its players. The same is true for the family. We may get frustrated by family members who seem so unlike ourselves, but the truth is, our team is made stronger because of the individual personalities brought to the family playing field.

Personality Inventory

A personality inventory that I do with all my English classes is what is known as the shape test. Take a look at the shapes below and circle the one to which you are most drawn.

Now see if the following interpretation of the shape you chose seems to match with your personality.

SQUARE

These folks are all about rules and order. Unlike many of their peers, they don't mind rules and actually enjoy having some kind of parameters in place. As children, they obey rules and are sometimes obnoxious as they attempt to make everyone else follow the rules, too. As students, they raise their hand after every assignment, clarifying the guidelines and expectations. As adults, they are often teased by others about having OCD issues. The clothes in their closets are organized by color, and a to-do checklist is always within reach.

CIRCLE

Circles are all about peace, love, and harmony. They value relationships and consider people to be much more important than tasks. Circles abhor conflict and will avoid it at all costs. Others know them as the peacemakers and encouragers. They enjoy being a part of a team and work hard to maintain friendships that could easily go to the wayside.

TRIANGLE

The triangles are often characterized by strong leadership traits. They are interested in progress and will do what they can to see that progress is made. These individuals are easily recognized by their peers and are often placed and voted into positions of authority. Even if they aren't chosen the leader, triangles will eventually assert themselves as leaders, determining that if they don't assume the role of leader, nothing is going to get done.

SQUIGGLE

As you've probably guessed, squiggles are unpredictable. You never know what they are going to say or do next. They may not always be the most dependable people, but their personalities make them fun to be around and the life of every party. If you had to describe a squiggle in one word, it would be "Squirrel!" They are high energy, highly charismatic, and highly likely to try the stunts that clearly bear the warning, "Never try this at home."

Q&A: *Did you successfully make a match? If not, which shape best describes you?*

The chances are not everyone in your family can be identified by the same shape. Take a moment now to consider each member of your family. Write their names under the shape that best describes them.

As we mentioned earlier, diversity is good, even in a family. The healthiest of families may have someone that exhibits characteristics of each of these shapes. For instance, everyone needs a good square in the family, someone who can update a calendar and organize events. My family often rolls their eyes at this mom for my insistence on an agenda for family vacations, but when I'm on the trip, we seldom miss an important tourist attraction, and we never find ourselves searching after dark for a vacant hotel room. Every family needs a circle, someone who listens, nurtures, and sacrifices for others. Sure, we may grow weary of their Kumbaya mentality and grow impatient when they promote peace rather than take our side in a situation, but they are the first we go to with our successes and failures. They truly care. A healthy family needs a triangle, someone who is not afraid to make decisions and take the blame if those decisions don't work out well. As a triangle himself, Bentley can come across a bit bossy at times, but as our leader, he has encouraged our whole family to grow spiritually. For that, we can put up with a bit of bossy. No family is complete without a squiggle. Fun moments together provide for a stronger family. While it is easy for the other shapes to get frustrated with the unpredictable, often unreliable, nature of their squiggle, they would still have to admit that the squiggle is certainly missed when he/she is not around. Life is never dull with a squiggle in the family.

To gain a fuller understanding of and appreciation for the members of your family, take a moment to answer the following questions and be ready to share your assessment with one another.

Q&A: *What is the most important contribution you make to your family's life?*

How does each member of your family contribute to your family's dynamic?

Which shape/personalities can you see might have a tendency to clash and why? Is this sometimes true in the personalities in your family?

We hope this exercise was both fun and enlightening. Even though your family, like ours, is made up of less-than-perfect people leading less-than-perfect lives, it is made stronger when we recognize and appreciate the contributions each member makes.

Along with these distinct personalities, your family also shares a unique culmination of past events and memories. Every semester, I have my English students write about an event from their childhood. Many of these compositions focus on family vacations and the memories that were made. Tales of camping trips, amusement parks, and sandy beaches fill their pages. While references are made to the destinations themselves, the majority of the writings focus on the memories made with their not-so-normal family members. I feel somewhat like a stalker as I read and laugh about the antics and adventures of these families I've never met. Grading these accounts is a highlight of my semester.

Q&A: *What about you? Did your family take vacations, and if so, what were some of your most memorable ones?*

Other submissions focus on holidays and family gatherings and the traditions that accompany them. Talk about unique.

One family I read about would gather a few days before Christmas to catch and wring the necks of chickens that would soon become the holiday meal. I've heard of the hanging of the greens but never the wringing of the necks. Traditions are a healthy part of any family, creating a sense of bonding and belonging as members become part of the sacred rituals of their particular group.

Q&A: Does your family have any traditions that revolve around New Year's, Easter, Thanksgiving, Christmas, or other holidays?

Many of the essays focus not only on the students' immediate family but also on members of the extended family, such as grandparents, aunts, uncles, and cousins. These extended family members are often identified in another essay I require entitled, "My Three Greatest Influences." Whether it is putting food on the table, offering words of wisdom, or providing an example of courage, family members are frequently cited as doing their part in influencing.

Q&A: Which of your family members, immediate or extended, have been the most influential in helping you become the person you are today?

It goes without saying that our family is a big reason we are who we are today. Not only did they pass along DNA and good looks, but they also helped us form opinions about important topics such as religion, education, and politics. Our family first introduced us to differences between right and wrong and helped us establish a moral compass. This group of people influenced our priorities and practices. Sometimes it was through positive examples; other times it may have been through negative ones.

Let's talk about the negative for a minute. While we have already established that all of our families are dysfunctional to one degree or another, some have experienced more than their fair share of atrocities, either through unwise decisions or uninvited life circumstances. This can result in deep hurt and/or emotional trauma. If left undealt with, these experiences can result in a victim mentality or hostility. According to Scripture, a more beneficial way of dealing with our negative family experiences is to learn something valuable from them.

Take a moment to read Ezekiel 18:10-17. According to verse 14, what does the wise son do with the negative example in his family?

While it is easy and even natural to hold a grudge, remain hurt, or become angry over negative examples in your family, it is much healthier to learn from the mistakes of others so that you and your future family will benefit from those experiences. Allow God to turn tragedies into triumph and a victim into a victor. Every experience is an opportunity to make you a stronger person.

Q&A: What are the most important lessons you have learned from your family, through either positive or negative examples, that you want to take into your own family someday?

God's Plan for the Family

Many young people have become disenchanted with the idea of family. While they love the idea of falling in love, they hesitate about making any commitment because they are not sure the idea of family can actually work. With 40-50 percent of marriages ending in divorce, the younger generation is looking for options other than a legal and binding marriage, yet the family has always been God's plan for populating the earth and making Himself known.

POPULATION

The family was the first institution created by God. In that glorious Genesis 2 moment when God brings Eve to Adam, God establishes a family, declaring that "a man shall leave his father and mother and be joined to his wife, and they shall become one flesh" (Gen 2:24). God blessed them and gave them the mission of having children and populating the earth. God looked at this family He had created and declared it very good. His plan for populating the earth is still working today.

REVELATION

The family would also become the primary means for making sure that all generations know that there is a God in heaven. Deuteronomy 6 is called the Shema, which means hear, listen, and witness.

Look closely at Deuteronomy 6:4-9. Who is responsible for making sure children hear, listen to, and witness the commandments of God? When and how is this to be done?

The family is God's Plan A for passing along the truths of His existence and His involvement with mankind. Sure, God did institute the church, but His first choice for making Himself known is through the family. The family as designed by God is the place where questions about God are asked and answered 24/7 (Deut 6:20). The ideal situation is a family where the parents are engaged in a growing and daily relationship with God, and they love and teach their children from the overflow of that Divine relationship. The greatest gift that any parent can give to their children is a home where God is made recognizable.

Take a moment to read Malachi 2:15. Why does God allow a couple to bring children into this world?

A godly family is dependent first upon a godly marriage. This idea is clearly conveyed in the New Testament. In Ephesians 5, Paul advises husbands and wives to love, respect, and submit to one another. He quotes the Genesis 2:24 passage and explains the purpose of a strong Christian marriage is to properly reflect within the family and to the world the relationship between Christ and His bride. Marriage is more than having someone to share the bills with—it's not an economic convenience. Neither is it simply a way to avoid loneliness—it's not a physical convenience. The underlying mission of any marriage and family is to glorify God, making Him recognizable on a daily basis.

This generation is wise in hesitating to rush into marriage. God takes marriage seriously and places great value on the family. It is one of His favorite instruments to use in making Himself known to the world. Because of this, we can't give up on the family either. Done God's way, it can work and work well. To set us up for success, God has given us instructions through His Word to help us be a functioning part of healthy families.

And healthy families is our goal. Not perfect families, but healthy families both now and in the future. You desire to have a healthy family of your own someday? Our admonition to you is to do what you can to have as healthy of a relationship with your current family as possible. This will help your future family in more ways than you can imagine.

Creating Healthy Families

We were visiting with a young girl a few years ago who was frustrated with her family situation. She was a Christian but felt that her parents had fallen short of their responsibilities to create a God-honoring environment in her home. Repeatedly she would say, "I'll endure this family for the time being and do things differently when I get a family of my own." While her reasoning makes sense, it doesn't work. Whether you like it or not, your current family will be a big part of your future family. We have always told our children that when they marry a person, they also marry his or her family. Because this is true, one of the best things you can do for your future family is to have as healthy of a relationship as possible with your current family. God has not left us on our own to figure out how to do this.

HONOR YOUR PARENTS

There's a good chance that if you were raised in a Christian home or in church, one of the first verses you memorized was Exodus 20:12: Honor your father and mother. Even non-Christian parents find a way to quote this verse. As if making it one of the Ten Commandments wasn't enough, God also had Paul to reiterate these words in Ephesians 6:2, reminding us this is the first commandment with a promise "that it may be well with you and you may live long on the earth." This promise seems to have less to do with length of life and more to do with quality of life. Life seems more enjoyable when we are getting along with our parents.

The Hebrew word for *honor* is *kabod* which means "to give weight to someone." When we are young, this means doing what our parents say: cleaning our room, finishing homework, staying out of the road. As we get older, it involves not only our actions but our attitudes. This means honoring our parents to their faces and behind their backs. It means regarding their decisions even if we don't agree with them. It means respecting the *position* of parent even if we find it challenging to respect the *actions* of our parent.

Read Ephesians 6:1-3. Does there seem to be any time limit on this? Any conditions?

The responsibility to honor parents appears to be a life-long one. Even after they have passed away, it is possible to honor them with our words and actions. The only condition we have found concerning honoring parents is if their request is in direct opposition to the clearly revealed will of God. As authority figures in our lives, we are to submit to them unless what they are asking would dishonor God. Daniel and his friends, Peter and the apostles all taught the importance of submitting to authority figures until asked to choose the commands of men over the commands God (Dan 3:8-12, Dan 6:6-23, Acts 5:27-42). This appears to be the only time we can biblically dishonor our parents, and even then, we need to be prepared to face consequences that may follow.

Q&A: *What are some practical ways you can honor your parents at this point in your life?*

LOVE YOUR SIBLINGS

Whether you are as close as Zach and Cody or mortal enemies like Mufasa and Scar, you'll have to admit your siblings play a significant role in your life. For a moment, forget all the trouble your siblings got you into (after all, it was always their fault, right?) and think of a favorite memory you have of each sibling. Be prepared to share these with one another. If you are an only child, be prepared to share some of the positives and negatives of growing up without siblings in the house.

Q&A: *What are some favorite sibling memories?*

Much has been written about birth order and sibling personalities. Firstborn are typically described as competitive and somewhat controlling, middle children are characterized as people pleasers and class clowns, last born are labeled as spontaneous, free spirited and sometimes self-centered. According to psychologists, only children tend to be perfectionists and conscientious.

Q&A: Do you feel there is any validity to these birth order characterizations? Why or why not?

Families serve many purposes, one of the greatest being they provide us with a practice field for our faith. Between the leather covers of your Bible, you will find practical advice for relationships and life. The family is the most obvious place to test-drive the applications of Scripture. For instance, Matthew 28 encourages us to share our faith with others; the family is a great place to begin. Romans 12:18 challenges us to be at peace as far as it depends on us; the family is a great place to begin. Colossians 3:13 advises us to forgive one another; the family is a great place to begin. James 3 urges us to tame our tongues; the family is a perfect place to begin. Think of any biblical principle and no doubt you will find a way that you can apply it to and practice it on your own family.

Q&A: What Bible verse or biblical principle do you need to practice on your family right now?

You may not have had the privilege of choosing whom your family would be, but God has placed you in your family for specific reasons. Make it your life-long goal to discover and enjoy those reasons. Families were designed by God to be a blessing; do what you can to be a blessing to and with your family right now, understanding that the healthier your personal relationship with your family is now, the healthier your relationship with your future family will be. It will be well worth the sacrifices of time and energy when you can introduce your future spouse to your imperfect, far from normal, but uniquely-yours family.

Keeping it Real with Nick and Samantha

Involving our families in our dating lives is a wise move on our parts. It may take a little coordinating of schedules, but why not try one of the following ideas to show your families that you haven't forgotten them?

- Plan a game night together. Game nights require little money and are always in season. You may choose a familiar game such as Dominoes, Yahtzee, or Uno, or you may want to be adventurous and introduce a new game. A good Spades, Spoons, or Bunco tournament will make for a lively evening. Make sure that you partner up with other members of the family and are not always competing against them as a couple. The idea here is to build family relations, not run-rule the folks. ☺
- Ice cream runs are always fun. Invite the family to jump in the car and join you for a double dip ice cream cone and great conversation. At Christmas time, get the ice cream to go and embark on a quest to find the prettiest lights in town.
- If your family enjoys the outdoors, plan a fishing outing at a nearby pond or lake. Who caught the biggest and smallest fish will still be the topic of conversation weeks later.
- Consider doing a random act of kindness for your family. Don some old clothes and wash their cars, clean the yard, or cook an amazing spaghetti dinner.

There's nothing like hearing your parents or siblings bragging on your choice of boyfriend/girlfriend. This is always more likely to happen when they can see the two of you interacting together and with them. Do what you can to show the family you care.

Making the Most of Your Meaningful Conversation

1. Which popular TV/movie family did you indicate best depicts your own and why?

2. Have you ever wondered whether your family is normal? Can you remember a time in the past or recently when this question came to mind?
   What are some of the quirks and idiosyncrasies that show up in your family?

3. Discuss with one another the shape test.
   - What shape best represents you?
   - What are the most important contributions you make to your family as this shape?
   - Which shapes best represent the rest of your family and how does each member contribute to the family's dynamic?
   - Which shape/personalities can you see might have a tendency to clash and why? Is this sometimes true of the personalities in your family?

4. Did your family take vacations, and if so, what were some of your most memorable ones?

5. Does your family have any traditions that revolve around New Year's, Easter, Thanksgiving, Christmas, or other holidays?

6. Which of your family members, immediate or extended, have been the most influential in helping you become the person you are today?

7. What are the most important lessons you have learned from your family, through either positive or negative examples, that you want to take into your own family someday?

8. What are some practical ways you can honor your parents at this point in your life?

9. What are some favorite sibling memories?

10. Do you feel there is any validity to these birth order characterizations? Why or why not?

11. What Bible verse or biblical principle do you need to practice on your family right now?

Chapter 8:

Friends

In your opinion, which of these TV/movie characters had the greatest friendship of all times?
   a) Frodo & Sam (*Lord of the Rings*)
   b) Dory & Marlin (*Finding Nemo*)
   c) Donkey & Shrek (*Shrek*)
   d) Andy & Barney (*Andy Griffith Show*)
   e) other: _____

Think back to some of the craziest stunts you have ever pulled. Chances are, you didn't pull them alone. Somewhere nearby there was a so-called friend with a twinkle in his eye or a lilt in her voice as they chanted, "Do it! Do it! Do it!" So against your better judgment, you crawled onto the world's most terrifying roller coaster, ordered the 150-ounce steak, or tried out a corny pick-up line on a good-looking stranger in the mall. There's something about being with friends that brings out the dauntless side of us. Friends make life fun. Perhaps this is what makes friendship the plot for many movies and TV shows, friendships that require the sacrifice of personal ambitions, romance, even life. We watch in awe as these friendships tug at our hearts' strings and stir up something inside of us that longs for such a bond. Take for instance these lines from A.A. Milne's *The House at Pooh Corner:*

> Piglet sidled up to Pooh from behind.
> "Pooh!" he whispered.
> "Yes, Piglet?"
> "Nothing," said Piglet, taking Pooh's paw. "I just wanted to be sure of you."

Even forty-something-year-old adults read those lines and empathize with Piglet. We want someone we can be sure of, a friend who knows everything about us and likes us regardless.

Q&A: Do you think there is something in all of us that longs for a friend? When do you think that longing is the strongest?

Like family, a friend is difficult to define. Merriam-Webster settled on "one attached to another by affection or esteem; a favored companion." The Free Dictionary by Farlex defines friend as "a person whom one knows, likes, and trusts." These and other definitions seem to be too generic in nature; they fall short of being able to encapsulate all the value and beauty of a friend. Pooh is more than a person Piglet knows, likes, and trusts. Chances are, your friends are more, too.

Evolution of Friendship

Perhaps so much is written about the topic of friendship because these are the second level of relationships we enter into after bonding with family. Whether it be through daycares, play dates, or church nurseries, children are soon introduced to other little humans who do not share the same bloodline. Thus begins an evolution of friendship that seems to change with different stages in life. Allow the next few pages to take you down a memory lane you can share with one another. Your friendships are an important part of who you are today.

EARLY CHILDHOOD FRIENDS

These first friendships are usually based on *convenience*. We find ourselves with others close in age because our parents are friends or we have the same caregivers. It is through these early friendships that we learn the hard lessons that the world doesn't revolve around us, and we are expected to share with others. School often becomes a practice field for these truths, and we begin forming friendships again out of convenience with children in our same classroom or neighborhood. We don't necessarily spend a lot of time choosing who will be our friends; this seems to be dictated by who is handy for a game of Tag or Hide and Seek.

Q&A: *Describe one of your earliest friendships. What made it special? What is one of the funniest adventures you got into with an early childhood friend?*

ADOLESCENT FRIENDS

As we grow a little older, our friendships move from being based on convenience to being based on *commonalities*. It doesn't matter so much whether we share a homeroom; we can always meet up at lunch break or after school. At this stage, it is more important that we have similar interests. Maybe we are on the same sports team or play in the middle school band. Perhaps we enjoy reading the same books, watching the same movies, or playing the same video games.

Q&A: *Who were your closest friends during the middle school years or ages 11-15? What are a few of your greatest memories involving friends during this time in your life?*

LATER TEENS

We gave the years from 16-19 a classification all their own. With a driver's license in hand, friends can now be chosen based on *camaraderie*. Our new mobility allows us to choose comrades from other schools, cities, and states. We find ourselves being drawn to certain personality types. Commonalities are still important, but we can cross clique lines if our personalities blend well. Sometimes we discover opposites can attract even in friendships. These friendships can be extremely influential as we continue developing a set of morals, values, and beliefs.

Q&A: *Who were/are your closest friends during the high school years or ages 16-19? What are some of your fondest memories? How did/do these friendships shape your personality?*

INTO ADULTHOOD

The late teen years can be both an exhilarating and educational time with friends. We learn the value of a faithful friend as opposed to a flattering one, and our standards for friendship become more *character-based* as we move into adulthood. We still long for crazy adventures with a sidekick, but virtues like honesty, loyalty, and dependability become greater factors in close relationships. We begin to realize our reputation is linked to those we run around with, and for the first time, that begins to matter. We've watched and experienced enough to recognize the truth of Proverbs 13:20: "He who walks with wise men will be wise, but the companions of fools will be destroyed." Somewhere along the way, we develop our list of characteristics we feel are most important in a true friend.

Q&A: *What characteristics show up on your "true friend" list? Which ones do you consider most important and why?*

Q&A: *Who would you consider to be your closest friends at this point in your life? What makes your friendship special? Do these friendships seem more based on character than friendships in the past?*

Every once in a while, a childhood friendship survives the evolution process and bridges the transition through adolescence into adulthood. These friendships are rare indeed. I (Susan) happen to be blessed with several of these, one dating to the early days of kindergarten when Tammy and I bonded in the play-kitchen corner and told the teacher we were allergic to grass so that we could stay inside and "bake" more sweets. Our wise teacher honored our sneezes and let us stay inside, and made us spend the next thirty minutes working boring, little kid puzzles. As tragic as that moment was, Tammy and I began a friendship, however seeped in deception it might have been, that remains strong to this day. We've maintained a Lucy and Ethel kind of friendship for over forty years and still have an annual slumber party with several of our Class of '86 chicks. British author Alexander McCall Smith writes, "You can go through life and make new friends every year-every month practically-but there was never any substitute for those friendships of childhood that survive into adult years. Those are the ones in which we are bound to one another with hoops of steel" (*The No. 1 Ladies' Detective Agency*).

Q&A: *Are you still close to any of your early childhood friends? If so, what has made this friendship survive?*

As we discussed in the introduction of this book, technology has made the world a much smaller place. Through Facebook and Instagram, we can stay in touch with people we met years ago, people we may only meet once, and people we have never met. Ask William Scott Goldberg, who holds the Facebook title of most friends with an overwhelming 6,223 friends, which is amazing considering Facebookers are limited to 5,000 friends. Of course, it would be safe to say that Goldberg hasn't shared a cup of coffee with all 6,223 of these friends. A simple invite or accept keystroke has made making friends seem like an effortless process.

Q&A: Do you think social media has changed our view of friends? Has it made maintaining friendships easier or more challenging?

With an ever-widening circle of friends literally at our finger-tips, it may be beneficial to consider what many have called concentric circles of friends. This is based on the idea that you are naturally going to be closer to some individuals than others, and not all friends are of equal standing. There are several versions of this model, but we've chosen to divide ours into three circles: confidants, colleagues, and contacts.

CONCENTRIC CIRCLES OF FRIENDS

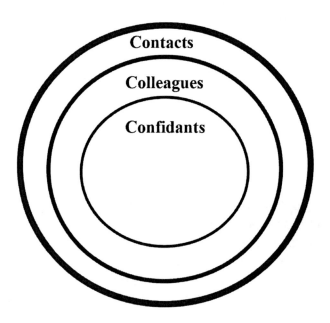

CONFIDANTS

These individuals are what you may describe as your true friends and kindred spirits. They have proven their allegiance by celebrating your victories and enduring your hardships and are what Proverbs 18:24 calls "a friend who sticks closer than a brother." You can share your deepest, darkest secrets and know those secrets will never become the source of gossip or bad-taste jokes. These are the friends you can call at 3 in the morning and know they won't push the ignore button on the phone. The relationship is marked by intimacy and honesty. Most people will share this kind of friendship with only one to five people over a lifetime. S.E. Hinton, author of *The Outsiders,* once wrote, "If you have two friends in your lifetime, you're lucky. If you have one good friend, you're more than lucky." The kind of good friend Hinton was referring to is this inner circle of the confidant.

COLLEAGUES

Since it would be unwise to place everyone we meet in the category of confidant, many of the people we associate with on a regular basis will enter into our colleagues circle. This circle can accommodate 5 to 100, depending on how socially active a person may be. Our colleagues are folks we share common interests with, perhaps in a work or school setting. We are on a first name basis, we enjoy their company, and we find the friendship to be beneficial. However, we would (and should) hesitate to expose all our vulnerable areas. Often these friendships dissolve if there is a change in the setting, such as a promotion, move, or new relationship.

CONTACTS

The vast majority of our friendships will fall into this third and outer circle. Contacts are more like acquaintances than soul mates. For whatever reason, our lives have crossed paths, and we have enjoyed an exchange of pleasantries. We may work together on a project, sip punch at an annual party, or have occasional run-ins at the local grocery store. We don't know the intricacies of one another's lives and are content with an amiable, surface relationship.

It may seem like a no-brainer that friends can fall into these different categories, but recognizing there are different levels of friendship has been an incredibly freeing revelation for me. I (Susan) love people and making friends. I love to find out their story and have more than once wept with a complete stranger. I love finding a common thread in the course of a conversation and weaving a tapestry. Because of this, I often find myself trying to push everyone into my inner circle, and this can be an unhealthy practice because with each level of friendship, there are different expectations.

For instance, we might expect a confidant to take off work and attend the funeral of our loved one, but we would never expect a contact to do so. We might excuse a colleague for forgetting our birthday, but confidants should remember it like their own. The closer the relationship, the greater the expectations. Therefore, it is inconceivable that we could treat every friendship like an inner circle, confidant relationship; we will wear ourselves out trying.

God made this clear to me a few months ago. A friend of mine shared some of her struggles with me. We prayed, studied the Word together, and sent lengthy text messages back and forth. We even celebrated when we saw God work in a mighty way. I guess that is why I was a bit disappointed when she failed to show any interest in a life-changing event going on in my life. I waited for her to ask questions, offer insight, or cheer me on. Nothing. That's when I received a friendship epiphany from God. Suddenly I realized that I thought this friend and I had entered into the inner circle of confidants, but actually our relationship was more ministry related than mutual. Just because God had invited me to be a part of her life during a difficult time did not mean we *had* to be confidants. Understanding this allowed my expectations to become more realistic, and it bothered me less that she only came to me to discuss her situations. Ours was to be a colleague friendship, and I adjusted my expectations to this level. How about you? Have you been frustrated in any friendships lately? Could it be that you have unrealistic expectations for the level of friendship you share?

We see Jesus observing these concentric circles of friendship in His ministry. No doubt, He had more "friends" than William Goldberg; the feeding of the 5000 (plus women and children) would have easily moved Him into a record-breaking status. His contact circle included all those who witnessed and experienced His miracles and teachings.

He invited others into His circle of colleagues. This would include the disciples, Mary, Martha, and Lazarus. He spent more time with these individuals, doing life and sharing moments.

But Jesus also had an inner circle, those with whom He invested a little more time and energy. There were some moments reserved for them alone.

To discover Jesus's inner circle, read the following passages:
- Mark 5:35-43
- Mark 9:2-9
- Matthew 26:37-46

Who were Jesus's confidants?

What can we learn from the way Jesus invested in friendships?

We can learn many lessons from the way Jesus dealt with the friends in His life, and a few are worth recapping. First of all, Jesus didn't share His deepest feelings with everyone. These thoughts were reserved for His inner circle. In the same way, our feelings and experiences are not meant to be broadcast to everyone. Social media is not always an appropriate place to voice what's on your mind. Some information is better off entrusted to a small group of confidants.

Secondly, Jesus invested the most time and energy in those to whom He was closest. It is often easy to neglect those in our inner circle because we feel confident they will always be there for us. Jesus never took His confidants and colleagues for granted. He invested Himself in their lives and allowed them to share in His.

Lastly, we can see from the Garden of Gethsemane scene that Jesus had a little higher expectations from those in His confidant circle. In His hour of greatest distress, He turned to God the Father but had hoped His closest friends would accompany Him to the throne. This didn't seem like an unrealistic request. When they didn't, Christ still honored the friendship; He died for them. Just as Christ understood the human frailty of Peter, James, and John, I want to be quick to forgive when my inner circle fails to meet my expectations. As wonderful as friends are, they are still human.

Luke 6:31 is an incredible verse to apply to all circles of friendship. As He wrapped up the famous Sermon on the Mount, Jesus admonished His followers to "Do unto others as you would have them do to you" (NIV). Somehow we have misinterpreted this verse to say, "Do to others as they have done to you," or "Do to others as you think they would do to you," but this is so far from Jesus's original intent. As our children were growing up, we would often make suggestions concerning their friendships. We might encourage them to check on someone who was sick or take a small gift on someone's birthday. Sometimes they would balk and claim, "But she never does that for me," or "He wouldn't do that for me." We would then remind our kids that we were never asked to treat others as they've treated us; we were asked to treat them the way we would like to be treated. This requires putting aside pride and a sense of entitlement and doing things God's way instead.

BIBLICAL BUDDY SYSTEM

There is something rewarding about honoring God through our friendships. After all, friends were His idea. The wisest man who ever lived once wrote, "Two are better than one, because they have a good reward for their labor. For if they fall, one will lift up his companion. But woe to him who is alone when he falls, for he has no one to help him up" (Ecc 4:9-10). God knew our treks through life would sometimes lead us through rocky terrain. Of course, He is there to be our Guide, but He often brings a fellow hiker alongside us to make the journey more enjoyable. Scripture is replete with examples and directives on how to make this buddy system work.

JOB AND FRIENDS

When studying the book of Job, we often focus on the first and last chapters, but a beautiful little jewel about friendship is snuggly embedded in the latter part of Chapter 2.

Read Job 2: 11-13. What did Job's friends do right?

Job's pals were doing everything right until they opened their mouths. Chapter 4 begins a 37 chapter long interrogation in which Job is in the hot seat, and his friends are begging him to confess his sins. The accusations only end because God steps in and silences the friends, declaring Job to be right and the friends guilty of an inaccurate interpretation of God. From this friendship fumble, we learn that words are not always necessary. Sometimes simply being there is enough.

A few years ago, a friend's father died in a terrible accident. I prayed that God would give me something profound and encouraging to pass along, but after several hours, He hadn't, and I knew I had waited long enough to touch base with my friend. I called and simply said, "I'm so sorry. I wanted to have something encouraging to say, but I've got nothing. I'm so sorry." We cried together, I told her I loved her, and we hung up. Later she shared with me how much that "nothing" meant. Evidently she was getting advice and explanations from many different directions and was exhausted from having conversations. To shed a few tears with a speechless friend was what she needed. We should never hesitate to simply be there for a friend; sometimes that means more than words.

Can you think of a time when words weren't necessary, and a friend's presence spoke volumes?

JONATHAN AND DAVID

Perhaps the most famous of Bible friendships, the story of Jonathan and David is one of selfless giving. Jonathan, son of Saul and natural heir to the throne, set aside any personal agenda and celebrated David's anointing from God even though it would cost him the title of King. He jeopardized his relationship with his father and his life to honor God through his friendship with David. He did so expecting nothing in return.

Can you think of a time when a friend put your needs before his/her own, expecting nothing in return?

For years, I assumed David and Jonathan's friendship ended when Jonathan, along with his father and two brothers, were slain by the Philistines on Mount Gilboa (1 Samuel 31). But the story of their friendship picks back up in 2 Samuel 9.

According to 2 Samuel 9, how did Jonathan and David's friendship continue?

Even when Mephibosheth's loyalty to David is brought into question a few chapters later, David continues to honor Jonathan through ongoing provisions. David continued to honor the covenant of friendship as long as he lived.

BARNABAS, PAUL, AND JOHN MARK

We first meet Barnabas in Acts 4 when he sells his land, gives the profits to the newly formed church, and is identified as the "Son of Encouragement." A few chapters later in Acts 9, he amazes us again by bringing a displaced Saul into the disciples' circle. The friendship grows as Barnabas and Paul minister in Antioch and are chosen for a mission project in Asia Minor. Barnabas invites a young cousin of his, John Mark, to come along, but for some reason unknown to us, John Mark decides to return home before the trip is complete. Paul and Barnabas seem to be doing fine until a second mission trip becomes the topic for discussion.

Read Acts 15:36-41. What happened to the friendship? Is it clear who is right and who is wrong?

Even the best of friendships can become fractured. Sometimes there is a clear right and wrong, but often the issue may be gray, and there may be room for right and wrong on both ends. The important lesson to learn from Paul and Barnabas is that a fracture doesn't have to be a finale'.

Read Colossians 4:10-11. What does knowing that Paul wrote this letter some fifteen years after the events in Acts tell you?

According to 2 Timothy 4:11, what is Paul's request about five years later from a dark, damp Roman prison?

Read 1 Peter 5: 13. As he nears the end of his life, how does Paul refer to the very John Mark whom he once refused to take on his second missionary journey?

Our friendships will be stronger when we realize that confrontation is not always bad, and fractures don't have to be final. We don't always have to agree. The Greek historian and biographer Plutarch once wrote, "I don't need a friend who changes when I change and nods when I nod; my shadow does that much better." A similar truth is conveyed in Proverbs 27:5-6:Better is open rebuke than love that is concealed. Faithful are the wounds of a friend, but deceitful the kisses of an enemy.

What do you think this Proverb means?

God never indicated maintaining healthy friendships would be easy, but like so many other things in life that involve pain, friendships are worth it. That's why we encourage you to make your friendships a priority even as your relationship with one another is developing. Too many times, couples become so engrossed in one another that they begin to alienate themselves from friends. Everybody seems to notice this except the couple themselves, and this never has a happy ending.

Let's say for some reason the couple breaks up. The separation is ten times worse because ties with former friends have been all but severed, and it is difficult to pick those friendships back up where they were left off.

Let's say the couple stays together and decides to enter into the blissful domain of marriage. If they have isolated themselves from friends, the joy of rounding up bridesmaids and groomsmen becomes a chore, and friends fulfill the duty knowing they will soon be pushed into the background again. Now, we're not suggesting that you need to spend time with friends so you can have a robust wedding party; we've just watched it play out before our eyes time after time where couples that isolate themselves from friends eventually feel, well, isolated themselves. Determine to do better with your friendships.

One way you can avoid this pitfall is to encourage one another to maintain and enjoy healthy friendships, especially with those that appeared in the confidant circle. Girls, you want to bring a smile to your guy's face? Encourage him to hang out with his buddies with your blessing. No guilt trip, no blackmail. Let him know that you see his friends as an important part of his life, and you don't view them as competition. If you do, pray that jealousy away; nothing is less attractive than an obsessive, smothering girlfriend. By understanding his need for healthy friendships, you'll find that you not only score points with your guy, but his bros will decide you may be good for him.

Guys, as much as she says she just wants to spend time with you, she needs to spend time with the girls. Encourage her to make a call to that childhood friend. Offer to double-date with her best friend. Make sure she is not neglecting the friendships that have shaped her into the incredible lady you enjoy spending time with today.

We would issue a word of warning concerning friends of the opposite sex. As your relationship with one another progresses, you will want to focus more on friendships of the same sex. While girl-guy friendships can be extremely successful and beneficial, they can cause a justified jealousy as a more romantic relationship enters the picture. Be sensitive, asking how you would feel if your date often made references to someone of the opposite sex and spent time with him or her on a regular basis.

Q&A: What can you do to help one another maintain healthy friendships?

The bottom line is that God rewards those who seek to honor Him through healthy friendships. Friends are often His means of comforting the discouraged, strengthening the weak, celebrating the good, and instigating the adventure. He uses friends to make us better than what we are alone. Proverbs 27:17 reminds us, "As iron sharpens iron, so a man sharpens the countenance of his friend."

If, while reading this chapter, you realize that you lack good friends, don't give up. Pray that God will bring someone into your life, then begin looking for opportunities to be the kind of friend you desire. Show an interest in the lives of others, and you may be surprised at the friendships that emerge. Dale Carnegie once said, "You can make more friends in two months by becoming interested in other people than you can in two years by trying to get other people interested in you." He was simply echoing a familiar Bible verse that says, "A man who has friends must himself be friendly" (Prov 18:24). As God brings special people into your life, resolve now to invest the time and energy appropriate for making the friendship one that is beneficial for both parties and join the ranks of Frodo and Sam, Donkey and Shrek, and Andy and Barney.

Keeping it Real with Nick and Samantha

It is easy to forget everyone else when you fall in "like" with someone, but keeping your friendships going is important. You can never have too many people to talk to, and if things don't work out, you will still be able to turn to your friends.

When we began dating, we set some friend boundaries that aided in the building of trust in our relationship. While we maintained friendships with the opposite sex, we limited the activities and time we shared with those friends. We agreed not to share with our friends each other's personal stories or anything that could later prove embarrassing for the other person. And we also decided it would be best when seeking relationship advice, to seek it from our more mature Christian friends. These boundaries helped so much.

With good friend boundaries in place, it is easier to encourage each other to spend time with friends. It can even be fun. Think of something you'd like to do with your friend(s). Set a day/night when you both spend time with your own compadres; then plan to share about it on your next date together. It will be fun to compare stories and relay details.

If your boyfriend/girlfriend has an amazing friend, why not make it a point to thank him/her for being such an important part of your guy/girl's life? Good friends are never competition; they are gifts that make life more enjoyable. Taking the time to appreciate and get to know each other's friends will only make your relationship with one another stronger.

Making the Most of Your Meaningful Conversation

1. Which TV/movie characters do you feel had the greatest friendship of all times?

2. Do you think there is something in all of us that longs for a friend? When do you think that longing is the strongest?

3. Describe one of your earliest friendships. What made it special? What is one of the funniest adventures you got into with an early childhood friend?

4. Who were your closest friends during the middle school years or ages 11-15? What are a few of your greatest memories involving friends during this time in your life?

5. Who were/are your closest friends during the high school years or ages 16-19? What are some of your fondest memories? How did/do these friendships shape your personality?

6. What characteristics show up on your "true friend" list? Which ones do you consider most important and why?

7. Who would you consider to be your closest friends at this point in your life? What makes your friendship special? Do these friendships seem more based on character than friendships in the past?

8. Are you still close to any of your early childhood friends? If so, what has made this friendship survive?

9. Do you think social media has changed our view of friends? Has it made maintaining friendships easier or more challenging?

10. What did you learn from each of the following?
    - Jesus and His circle of friends
    - Job and his friends
    - Jonathan and David
    - Barnabas, Paul, and John Mark

11. What can you do to help one another maintain healthy friendships?

Chapter 9:

Physical Fitness

When it comes to my physical well-being, I'm
    a) a health nut.
    b) a health not.
    c) full of good intentions.
    d) waiting on the new, glorified body promised in Scripture.

*M*ost of us can easily identify health nuts with their tight-fitting athletic wear, hydro flasks, and fitness trackers. Their ability to climb three flights of stairs without being winded, eat something as colorless and tasteless as tofu, and make a ponytail look stylish leave the majority of us wrestling with a good amount of guilt and envy. But according to the statistics, health NOTS still rule. In 2005, a study was published by Live Science Staff, revealing that a mere 3 percent of Americans are living a genuinely healthy lifestyle.[8] The study, which involved 153,000 adults from all 50 states, focused on four basic criterion for being physically fit:

- Non-smoking
- Maintaining a healthy weight (body mass index)
- Consuming 5 or more fruits and vegetables per day

- Engaging in regular physical activity defined as at least 30 minutes 5 times per week

Q&A: *Based on the above criteria, are you living a healthy lifestyle? If not, where is your greatest struggle?*

With all the products, programs, and pilates available, you would think that our nation would be stepping up its game in the physical arena; however, an April 2015 report by Dr. Michael Greger suggests the percentage has dropped to 1%, or 1.2% to err on the side of liberality.[9]

Q&A: *Why do you think individuals as a whole are less healthy today than they were ten years ago?*

For the average chocolate lovers like ourselves, we have to ask the question of whether physical fitness is really that important. After all, aren't we to be more interested in the spiritual realm than the physical? Aren't all good gifts from above, and wouldn't that include chocolate cupcakes? We can make all the arguments we want, but 1 Corinthians 6:19-20 continues to stand like a treadmill in a gym, reminding us that our bodies are the temples of the Holy Spirit, and we are therefore to honor God with them.

Lest we all quit our day jobs and take up residency in the gym, we need to realize Scripture also comes with a warning of becoming overly obsessed with health matters. Read 1 Timothy 4:7-8. What seems to be Paul's message for Timothy in these verses? What is Paul's reminder to us?

Q&A: *Do you think it is possible to become obsessed with physical fitness? What does this look like and how can one guard against it?*

Paul, through the divine inspiration of the Holy Spirit, confirms that taking care of this temple, tent, jar of clay God has entrusted to us does have value. Our purpose for doing so should be more tied to honoring God than building abs. If our motivation for becoming physically fit is simply swimsuit season or Facebook photos, the focus is more on honoring self than God. Perhaps a more godly approach to staying physically fit is that of Jim Elliott who even before he knew of God's plan to send him to the Wadoni tribe of Ecuador, resolved to be in the best shape possible for whatever mission God gave him.

Most health experts agree on three areas that will help improve your physical health and appearance; we've added a couple more that will help as you determine to allow your body to become the temple of God Scripture declares it to be. Don't let the following questions send you on a guilt trip of any kind; instead, look forward to discussing these areas together and encouraging one another to find ways you may be able to work together toward a healthier lifestyle.

Honoring God with your Body

1. Eat Right.

Medical experts differ widely on their opinions of what constitutes a healthy diet. Some promote eating meats while others push a vegetarian agenda. While our goal is not to endorse a particular diet or pattern, we would encourage you to take a few minutes to objectively evaluate your eating habits.

Q&A: *Victor Lanlair once said, "You are what you eat." If this were true, what would you be?*

What is your greatest weakness in maintaining a healthy diet?

What changes in diet may you need to make to better honor God with your body?

2. Get Exercise.

While the experts seem to agree that 30 minutes of physical activity for 5 days a week is ideal, this may look different for each person and may change during various seasons of life. More than once the Freshman 15 has struck an unsuspecting college student who no longer has the demands of high school sports. The responsibility falls on us to find ways to retain physical activity in our daily lives.

Q&A: What forms of exercise are most appealing to you?

What changes in routine may you need to make to get more exercise?

3. Sleep well.

In 2015, an estimated 25 percent of the US population suffered from sleep deprivation.[10] Insufficient sleep is linked to chronic illnesses, mental conditions, and lower productivity. People often forfeit sleep, feeling it is a waste of time when in actuality, those hours of shut eye help improve our physical well-being and lend to a better quality of life when we are awake. Take a few minutes to do an Internet search on sleep tips and then tackle the questions below.

Q&A: How many hours of sleep per night do you generally need? Are you getting enough sleep?

What changes in routine may you need to make to get enough sleep? Did you find any sleeping tips that may be worth trying?

4. Practice good hygiene.

Not only will good hygiene help us avoid infectious disease, but it will also improve personal relations. Caring for the temple God has given us by maintaining good dental hygiene, bathing regularly, spending a little time on a presentable hairstyle, and battling odors of any kind will prove a benefit for us and others.

Q&A: Is it possible for hygiene to cross a line and become vanity, and if so, where is the balance?

Are there any changes you may need to make concerning your personal hygiene?

5. Dress appropriately.

While the medical experts won't mention clothing in an article about staying physically fit, we feel it is an important part of honoring God with the body. It is fun to express our individuality through styles and threads, and there are certainly plenty of choices out there. However, as walking temples of God, we should carefully choose what we wear so that it presents a positive image of who we are and Whose we are. Women are given a clear directive in 1 Timothy 2:9-10 to dress modestly, but the principle of dressing appropriately also applies to guys. It's important that our clothes send three messages: I respect myself, I respect others, and I respect God.

Q&A: Do clothes say that much about a person? What statements do your clothes make?

Do you need to make any changes where your wardrobe is concerned to honor God in this area?

The issue of appropriate apparel has become such a major issue in our culture that we will address it again in this chapter, giving you another opportunity to discuss how the two of you can best help each other in this area.

It also seems that this topic provides a perfect segue to the second half of this chapter. According to the Bible, another important facet of staying physically fit and honoring God with our bodies involves our sexuality. Yep, you knew we would have to go there eventually. It is our hope that the next few pages will guide you into a conversation that will allow you to discuss and set boundaries concerning the physical aspect of your relationship.

Perhaps no facet of the dating relationship is more exciting and at the same time challenging as that of physical intimacy. Almost weekly we listen to starry-eyed girls describe that tingly sensation when "his hand touched mine," or guys admit they remember nothing about the movie except what it felt like to finally get the nerve up to "slip my arm around her shoulders." Physical touch is a natural and expected part of any dating relationship, but what can a couple do to make sure God is included and honored through this aspect of the relationship? Does the Bible provide counsel for what is and isn't appropriate?

Sure, it does. God desperately wants His children to succeed in this area and has provided tutelage from Genesis through Revelation. We have found one of the key verses on the topic is the well-known Romans 12:1-2:

Therefore, I urge you, brothers, in view of God's mercy, to offer your bodies as living sacrifices, holy and pleasing to God—this is your spiritual act of worship. Do not conform any longer to the pattern of this world, but be transformed by the renewing of your mind. Then you will be able to test and approve what God's will is—his good, pleasing and perfect will. (NIV) According to verse 2, where does the process of presenting your bodies a living sacrifice to God begin?

The quest of honoring God with our bodies begins in our mind. Paul admonishes us to avoid conforming to the pattern of the world. To do so, we must first recognize that pattern. Take a few minutes to do so now.

Q&A: What does culture say about physical intimacy, dating, and sex?

We recently had this discussion with a group of 18-28 year olds. Using TV shows and movies as their primary evidence, they finally formulated one sentence that would sum up the prevailing voice of culture on the topic: Physical intimacy, including sex, is perfectly natural and acceptable and has few if any consequences or strings attached. Notice there is no limit on how many people can be involved, no mention of love, and no question about further intentions. In other words, anything goes. If this is the message being sent, it is no wonder that only 3 percent of Americans will wait until marriage to have sex.[11]

Q&A: Do you feel the small group accurately portrayed culture's view of physical intimacy, dating, and sex? Why or why not?

Biblically Transformed

After identifying culture's view, we are encouraged by Romans 12 to hold it up in the light of Scripture and allow it to be transformed. Take a few minutes to read the following verses and jot down in the provided space your thoughts on how God addresses this topic.

1. 1 Corinthians 6:9-11, 18-19

Many times we will have young people remind us that Exodus 20:14 forbids committing adultery but doesn't say anything about premarital sex; however, verse 11 of this passage in 1 Corinthians makes a distinction between the sexually immoral or fornicators (KJV) and adulterers. Adultery would be defined as sex in addition to a marriage. Fornication would be sex before marriage. Both are addressed as sex outside of marriage and contrary to God's will.

2. Hebrews 13:4

Note the reference to a marriage bed. A dating bed or engagement bed is never mentioned. The Bible seems to indicate that God's plan is for the marriage bed to be shared by only two people. Keeping it pure includes making good decisions before and during marriage.

3. Ephesians 5:25-27

Shortly after their wedding, we were discussing this passage with our daughter Samantha and her husband Nick. Nick said it was these verses that made him determined to keep their relationship physically pure. "Thinking that I was responsible for her purity made me more accountable. I wanted to present her to Christ as pure and radiant." Yep, he's a keeper.

4. Song of Solomon 3:5

It is important (and encouraging) to know that God doesn't say, "Don't have sex;" He simply says, "Wait until the right time." That right time appears to be within the confines of marriage.

Q&A: *What does Scripture say about physical intimacy, dating, and sex?*

Most of us are familiar with these Scriptures, and for some, these words are enough to deter us from accepting culture's invitation to walk on the wild side. Others may still be questioning if God is serious about this issue. For the skeptics, God has carefully included the testimonies of two men who were faced with their own physical dilemmas.

MEET JOSEPH

Take a few minutes to read Genesis 39:6-10. What do you notice about Joseph's response to Potipher's wife?

Joseph was a remarkable young man. Scripture never says he wasn't tempted, but it records clearly that he refused because it was more important to him to please God than to please himself or another. Note that his fear of offending God was even greater than his fear of getting caught. It was his main motivation for refusing to cross physical boundaries.

MEET DAVID

No doubt, you are familiar with this story, but take a few minutes to refresh your memory by reading 2 Samuel 11:1-5. What stands out to you most in these verses? Where did David go wrong?

1 Corinthians 10:12-13 offers a warning and a promise:
> Therefore let him who thinks he stands take heed lest he fall. No temptation has overtaken you except such as is common to man; but God is faithful, who will not allow you to be tempted beyond what you are able, but with temptation will also make the way of escape, that you may be able to bear it.

Was David's temptation unbearable? Did God provide him a way out? To David, his temptation may have *seemed* unbearable, but God provided him with a way out. At that moment, the man after God's own heart chose to love himself more than God. His testimony is a sober reminder that even those who love God can find themselves in the throes of temptation. To be tempted is not the sin; to refuse to handle it God's way is.

David dealt with the after effects of his one night fling for the rest of his life. His regrets are recorded in the chapters of 2 Samuel and several of the psalms. Joseph, on the other hand, endured some hardships because of his decision, but his story ends well. Apparently, Joseph never regretted his decision in Potipher's house. We never hear him saying, "Sure wish I'd taken Potipher's wife up on her offer. I missed out." We have found the same to be true during our years in college ministry. We have never had one of our students that waited come back and say, "I sure am sorry I waited," but we've dealt with many God-loving, young people who returned to say, "I sure wish I had."

For this reason, we encourage you, if you haven't already, to set some physical boundaries. If you've made it to this chapter in the book, it is obvious you are enjoying your time together and that you desire to honor God in your relationship. First, pray and ask God if this is a good time in the relationship to discuss boundaries. If He confirms that it is, then take the task at hand seriously, and enjoy working together to find a purity plan.

Some boundaries are obvious and will apply to any couple that desires to honor God, but we've noticed that God will actually ask some couples to live by even higher standards. We have known couples who felt led to refrain from kissing until they were engaged and one couple that actually waited to kiss at the wedding ceremony. Another couple never allowed themselves to be alone. Whatever boundaries you set, make sure they line up with the Word of God, are attainable with His help, and are set with the purpose of honoring Him.

To help with your process, we have provided some of the best advice we've collected from young people over the past twenty-five years.

Beneficial Boundaries

1. Stay Public.

You are less likely to find yourself in a compromising situation when there is a potential audience. Many couples refuse to be in a house or an apartment alone together. A college dormitory room may present the biggest challenge with its limited furniture. You may also want to consider a "No Parking" guideline. If you find as a couple you need a quiet place to sit and talk after dark, consider parking in a well-lit spot or a late night, fast food restaurant. Refuse to allow yourself to be set up for an intimate disaster in a secluded spot.

Q&A: Are there any boundaries you feel the need to set in regards to staying public?

2. Dress with Discretion.

Many times we send a message and set ourselves up for a compromising situation with the way we dress. Be sure to respect your date by choosing your attire carefully. After a day at the lake, one young man asked his girlfriend to wear a cover-up if they ever chose to go swimming again. Before she could get offended, he explained that he found her very attractive, but he wanted to honor and respect her with his mind and thoughts. This was difficult for him to do in such a skin-bearing setting. The same is true with revealing clothing. Guys tend to be visual, and you can imagine the frustration this must present for a young man who desires to honor God. Girls, let's help them by following the instructions given by Paul in 1 Timothy 2:8-10: "I desire therefore that...the women adorn themselves in modest apparel, with propriety and moderation, not with braided hair or gold or pearls or costly clothing, but, which is proper for women professing godliness, with good works." Guys, help us. Don't compliment us if we are wearing immodest clothing. Your compliment, no matter how well meant, will encourage us to wear immodest clothing again.

Q&A: *Is it important to dress for success rather than sexcess? Share with one another what might be helpful and what might detract from your goal of honoring God physically.*

3. Purpose to take things slowly.

Physical purity is not the norm, and it doesn't happen without two people being intentional. As awkward as it might be, have an honest discussion about displays of affection. Our daughter and son-in-law decided to wait until they had been dating six months before sharing a kiss. It was a challenge, but both agreed that it helped them learn more about one another rather than focusing on feelings. Other couples who choose similar commitments talk about how much more they can enjoy simple gestures like holding hands and an arm around the shoulder. We've known couples who set limits on the kind of kissing or hugging they would engage in. You may also want to discuss what is appropriate for public displays of affection. As long as both individuals know what to expect and share the same goal of a healthy relationship, purposing to take things slowly works. Don't worry about stifling the romance with such boundaries; romance is much more than physical touch.

Q&A: How important is it to you that the physical aspect of the relationship moves slowly? Discuss together what you feel would be appropriate and inappropriate displays of affection.

4. Stay vertical.

Let's be honest; some situations invite unplanned, passionate moments. One study suggests that only 17% of young women actually planned for their first sexual encounter; for the other 83% it sort of happened, often leaving a mound of regrets in the wake.[12] One way to avert such a moment is to determine to stay vertical. Avoid compromising situations such as napping together, lying on the couch together, wrestling, and sleeping over. Even if nothing happens, it eventually will for two people who are attracted to one another. These actions will also cause others to assume something is happening whether it is or not. In 1 Thessalonians 5:22, Paul reminds Christians to abstain from even the appearance of evil. Many young couples say staying vertical is helping them to avoid compromising situations.

Q&A: Does staying vertical seem like a good boundary for your relationship?

5. Invite accountability.

Most of the couples we see maintaining healthy relationships have found ways to hold themselves accountable. Some choose visual reminders, such as a piece of jewelry, that speak of a commitment they have made to God. Others ask fellow believers they trust and respect to serve as accountability partners. Accountability partners may offer counsel about boundaries and ask questions about the relationship at any time. If you choose to have an accountability partner, we encourage you to choose someone of the same sex who is also seeking to honor God in his/her relationships.

Q&A: How might you invite accountability into your relationship?

Several years ago, Gary Chapman came out with a book entitled *The Five Love Languages* in which he suggested there are five main languages people speak when they are showing or receiving love. These include words of affirmation, acts of service, quality time, gifts, and physical touch.

Q&A: Which of these would you identify as your love language?

If your love language is physical touch, understand that your boundaries may have to be a bit more stringent. One night our daughter came home from a date with Nick feeling pretty rejected. While watching a movie, she had placed her hand on his leg. He patted it and set it back on her own and gently asked that she not put her hand on his leg. She interpreted his action to mean that he didn't find her attractive, but the opposite was true. Because physical touch was his love language and he found her attractive, Nick had to set definite boundaries out of respect for her and for God. By doing so, you can bet he earned our respect as well. That's the kind of guy every mom and dad want their daughter to date.

As we wrap up the topic of setting boundaries, it is important to note that doing so not only makes you more physically fit, but it will improve your spiritual and emotional health as well. The worst break ups we have witnessed were those where the couple had gone too far physically. This makes sense since sex is not just physical. There is a bonding that takes place, and a break up after such bonding can lead to severe trust issues. Despite what culture teaches, sex outside of the biblical parameters of marriage affects a person's total well-being. The guilt that often accompanies premarital and extra-marital sex certainly takes its toll on an individual's body, mind, and spirit.

Many of you reading this can give personal testimony. In a moment, boundaries were abandoned, and passion won out. Does the Bible have any advice for those who have awakened love before its time? Take a moment to reread 1 Corinthians 6:9-11, focusing on the verb used four times in verse 11.

Q&A: What would you say to someone who was no longer a virgin and is wondering whether they can reclaim their sexual purity?

If you have struggled with sexual purity, at some point you may need to discuss past relationships with one another. We encourage this honesty about the past when the dating relationship has reached a safe level and before it reaches a secure level. Sharing information about the past can make a person feel extremely vulnerable, and this information shouldn't be entrusted to everyone you date. By *safe*, we mean that you have developed a level of trust with one another and your relationship seems to be progressing in a positive direction. *Secure* indicates some kind of commitment such as an engagement. Sharing about the past needs to happen sometime between safe and secure. While the conversation may not be an easy one, it is certainly one that is better to have at the forefront of marriage instead of afterward. Failing to do so will set your current relationship up to be haunted by guilt and secrets.

While you may not be able to change your past, understand that you can improve your future by making good decisions in the present. This relationship that you are in right now could begin setting a new standard for healthy dating. As you consider becoming more physically fit and devise a purity plan, keep in mind the whole purpose of dating is to glorify God and discover His will in a specific relationship. He is inviting you to use this relationship to show a watching world what it looks like to have a healthy, God-centered relationship. As you seek to honor Him, you will discover the freedom that comes with making good choices. Recently, one of our students was discussing a break up she had just experienced. We expected her to be disappointed, and maybe she was a little. But more than anything, she was elated the relationship had been marked by good choices and physical fitness. With a smile on her face she exclaimed, "Finally, I was in a relationship that I didn't have to walk away from saturated in guilt because of lines we had crossed."

May her testimony be yours as you seek to honor God and stay physically fit in your relationship.

Keeping it Real with Nick and Samantha

Early in our dating relationship, we expressed our mutual desire to remain sexually pure. We established several of the guidelines discussed in this chapter, including staying public and taking things slowly. Many of our dates involved other people; even when we were alone, we would make sure that others were within eyesight or earshot. Perhaps the most helpful tip we can offer in the quest for staying physically pure is to settle on short goodbyes and hand holding prayers at the end of each date; these go a long way in helping you fulfill your God-given responsibilities in the fight against temptation.

At times, all our endeavors seemed a bit extreme, but looking back, it was certainly worth the extra effort. Our relationship today is stronger because of decisions we made during those 2 ½ years of dating. It can be done; not everyone is "doing it," and you are not a freak for choosing to save that which is sacred. God's plan always results in greater physical, emotional, and spiritual health.

Making the Most of Your Meaningful Conversation

1. How did you answer the multiple choice question at the beginning of the chapter?

2. Based on the four criterion listed in the first paragraph, are you living a healthy lifestyle? If not, where is your greatest struggle?

3. Why do you think individuals as a whole are less healthy today than they were ten years ago?

4. Do you think it is possible to become obsessed with physical fitness? What does this look like and how can one guard against it?

5. If "you are what you eat," what would you be? What is your greatest weakness in maintaining a healthy diet? What changes in diet may you need to make to better honor God with your body?

6. What forms of exercise are most appealing to you? What changes in routine may you need to make to get more exercise?

7. Are you getting enough sleep? What changes in routine may you need to make to get enough sleep?

8. Is it possible for hygiene to cross a line and become vanity, and if so, where is the balance? Are there any changes you may need to make concerning your personal hygiene?

9. What statements do your clothes make? Do you need to make any changes where your wardrobe is concerned to honor God in this area?

10. What does culture say about physical intimacy, dating, and sex? What does Scripture say about physical intimacy, dating, and sex?

11. Discuss physical boundaries with one another. You may want to use the following suggestions as starting points: stay public, dress with discretion, purpose to take things slowly, stay vertical, invite accountability.

12. Which of Gary Chapman's love languages do you speak most loudly?

13. Is there something from your past that you need to share with one another? Do so only after praying and determining that your relationship is safe.

Chapter 10:

Reflection

Which song title best describes your current dating relationship?
   a) "A Whole New World" (from *Aladdin*)
   b) "A Groovy Kind of Love" (Phil Collins)
   c) "Danger Zone" (Kenny Loggins)
   d) "Beauty and the Beast" (from *Beauty and the Beast)*

For the past few months, you have worked through the pages of this book together, sharing details about your greatest fears, wildest dreams, and craziest family members and friends. Hopefully, it has been both an educational and a bonding experience. If you're still engaged in the study, then it's a sign that something positive has been happening in your relationship. In this final chapter together, we want to encourage you to take an honest look at where your relationship is and where to go from here. As American writer and management consultant Margaret Wheatley has declared, "Without reflection, we go blindly on our way, creating more unintended consequences, and failing to achieve anything useful."

Q&A: How long have the two of you been in a relationship? Overall, how do you feel the relationship is progressing?

Our guess is that most couples, regardless of how long they have been dating, would say the relationship has had its ups and downs but seems to be working. That's what we find when we ask the couples we come into contact with on our college campus. However, reflection on something as serious as whom you might spend the rest of your life with deserves more than one general question. We invite you to take a little closer look at the overall health of your relationship by examining it from four different angles: emotionally, socially, physically, and spiritually. Think of it like a toll road. To travel on the best roads, you occasionally have to pull up to a toll booth, roll down your window, and make a small investment. As you do, a light in front of you instructs you on what to do next. This little exercise is an investment of your time that will help you to know what is next.

Please begin this process with prayer. Since God is omniscient, He is the only one who knows where your relationship is heading, and it is His opinion that matters most. Ask Him to reveal truths to you so that you can evaluate and answer each question honestly. Don't try to throw the results by answering in such a way that the exercise is forced to declare you a perfect couple. Regardless of how much you like the other person, answer the questions as objectively as possible. We're not trying to make a 100%; this assignment is not for a grade. Like many class assignments, this exercise is simply to increase your understanding so that you can pass the test later when it really does matter.

Couple's Crossroads Exercise

Take a few minutes to score each statement on a scale from 1 to 5, with 1 being "Not really" and 5 being "Pretty much always." Answer as objectively as possible.

EMOTIONAL HEALTH

1. We avoid playing mind games and manipulating one another. 1 2 3 4 5
2. We do not always have to be together, and we avoid smothering one another. 1 2 3 4 5
3. We are honest and open with one another and communicate clearly. 1 2 3 4 5
4. When we do disagree, we can discuss the issue in a mature manner. 1 2 3 4 5
5. We encourage one another verbally and treat each other with respect when it is just the two of us. 1 2 3 4 5

SOCIAL HEALTH

1. We make a point to spend time with friends outside of one another. 1 2 3 4 5
2. We work at maintaining healthy relationships with our own families. 1 2 3 4 5
3. We work at maintaining healthy relationships with each other's families. 1 2 3 4 5
4. We choose entertainment that doesn't compromise our morals. 1 2 3 4 5
5. We treat each other with respect when others are around. 1 2 3 4 5

PHYSICAL HEALTH

1. We encourage each other to be physically fit and healthy. 1 2 3 4 5
2. We have set boundaries that determine our physical involvement. 1 2 3 4 5
3. We avoid compromising situations. 1 2 3 4 5
4. We dress in such a way as to show that we respect ourselves and one another. 1 2 3 4 5
5. We have established some measure of accountability. 1 2 3 4 5

SPIRITUAL HEALTH

1. We each have a consistent personal quiet time with God. 1 2 3 4 5
2. We can pray together and for one another. 1 2 3 4 5
3. We discuss spiritual things. 1 2 3 4 5

4. We are each involved in a local church. 1 2 3 4 5
5. We are involved in ministry opportunities. 1 2 3 4 5

Take a few minutes to total your score for each area and record it on the correct blanks below. Then draw a line from your points to traffic light color that fits with your score in each area.

Emotional Health _____

Social Health _____

Physical Health _____

Spiritual Health _____

RED
5-9

YELLOW
10-14

GREEN
15-25

You have to admit—traffic lights were a pretty nifty invention. They are strategically placed at intersections and crossings to help prevent accidents and to control traffic flow. Without them, traveling would be hazardous to say the least. These little 42" rectangles give a lot of direction and order to our lives and instruct us on what to do next. In the same way, the above exercise may offer some direction and instruction on how and when to proceed in your dating relationship.

Q&A: Pretend for a moment that you are paused at an intersection for your current dating relationship. What signals did you receive from the Couple's Crossroads Exercise, and how do you interpret those signals?

While it's pretty obvious what red, yellow, and green lights mean on a traffic light, let's spend a little time exploring what they mean in a dating relationship.

Red Lights

Considering the average person will date eleven people before marrying, it's safe to say that most people will at some point or another hit a red light in a relationship.

While one or more red lights definitely means STOP and evaluate, it could mean more. It may be this relationship is not healthy for one or both partners, and it's time for it to come to an end. This is never easy and can be downright awkward or traumatic, but sometimes a break up is the best thing that can happen for all parties involved. As painful as it can be, there are worse things than breaking up.

Some individuals are not convinced of this and will do everything they can to keep the relationship alive. A few semesters ago, we listened as a young girl shared the details of her unhealthy relationship. Even with all the red lights that were flashing, she desperately wanted to believe that this was the guy God would allow her to be with the rest of her life. She had experienced a painful break up in a previous relationship, and she didn't feel she could survive such angst a second time. She and her current boyfriend had crossed physical boundaries early in their relationship, and she somehow felt if they stayed together, this would be made right in marriage. Finally, the two of them had been together for over a year; to break up now would seem like a complete waste of time and emotions.

"But none of these are good enough reasons to stay together," you may be thinking. "Can't she see this relationship is not based on love?" She couldn't, or at least refused to admit it, and so do many others who like her are resigned to settle for less than God's perfect will because they are convinced that a break up equals failure. So we come full circle, back to the introduction of this book.

According to the second page of the Introduction, what is the purpose of dating?

Sometimes a break up is necessary in order for God's will for a person's life to be fully introduced. This was my experience. I (Susan) began dating an incredible young man when I was 16. He was committed to the Lord and serving the church when we met and began a 2 ½ year relationship. While it wasn't perfect, it was a healthy relationship; however, after our first year away at college, we began to wonder if it was God's best. We decided we would trust God with our futures. We would break up, and if He saw fit to bring us back together somewhere down the road, that would be up to Him. In the months and years afterward, God brought Bentley into my life and a beautiful, God-loving woman into his. Both of our families are now involved in ministry and occasionally run into one another at state events. While I still have the utmost respect for this man and the relationship we had, I know without a doubt that a break up was the only way God could introduce His perfect plan for both of our lives.

While most of us will agree that break ups can be blessings, we may differ in how we go about them. Whatever the timing and means, break ups should always be God-honoring. Is that even possible? According to Scripture, it is. Take a moment to write 1 Corinthians 10:31 in the space below.

According to Paul, all we do should be done for the glory of God. Two words stand out in this verse. *All* means everything, including break ups. Paul wouldn't ask us to do something impossible, so God-honoring break ups must be possible. The other word is *glory*, which means to make one recognizable. Even in our break ups, we can and should make God recognizable. Whether you are the one doing the breaking up or receiving the news, there are steps you can take to ensure a God-honoring, drama- reducing break up.

If you're the one breaking up:

1. *Spend some time in earnest prayer.*

James 1:5 encourages us to seek wisdom from God "who gives generously to all without finding fault, and it will be given you" (NIV). God can provide wisdom as to whether a break up is necessary, and He can provide wisdom on the best way to go about it. Pray it through so that the peace of God, which surpasses all understanding, will help you approach the situation with a right attitude. Make sure you are serious about wanting the break up. One of the most disastrous relationship practices is that of break up/make up. These often lead to break ups and make ups in marriage. One of the rules we made when we started dating was that we wouldn't break up unless we meant it. This eliminated the emotional roller coaster of break ups and make ups that many of our friends found themselves riding.

2. *Seek wise counsel.*

Proverbs 12:15 reminds us that a wise man listens to advice. Choose someone you consider wise, and talk with them about what you are planning to do. Sometimes hearing yourself talk out loud will help you weed through right and wrong things to say.

3. *Reduce the drama.*

It may be easier to text or simply make excuses as to why you are no longer available to go out, but the most God-honoring break ups involve a respectful, face-to-face conversation. You can also reduce the drama and confusion by being compassionate but honest. As tempting as it may be, don't offer a false hope of getting back together in the future. While this may seem kind on your part, it can prove detrimental to the other person, making it more difficult for them to move on.

4. Avoid blaming.

Accept responsibility for the break up. This is not the time to point out the faults of the other person or to blame them to their face or behind their back. Instead, focus on the relationship, not the person, speaking the truth in love and in words that build up and are fitting (Eph 4:29). Be careful not to blame a third person by saying something like, "I visited with so-and-so, and he/she felt like it was best if we break up." Also, avoid blaming God. Many times in an effort to ease the pain, a person will say, "I feel like God is asking me to call the relationship off." This can and often does result in the heartbroken blaming God, too.

5. Grieve the loss.

Out of respect for yourself, the other person, and your future relationship, don't jump back into another relationship quickly. Take some time to reflect and learn about relationships and yourself. While you do, stay off social media and guard your reputation. Flirting soon after breaking up will often result in the label of "player," and there's nothing God-honoring about that. God may even invite you to be a part of what many young people are calling a dating fast, where they commit to focusing on God rather than dating for a set amount of time.

While most of this seems like obvious advice, it's funny how common sense is the first thing that goes out the window when we want to avoid conflict or an awkward situation. If you're certain that a break up is the best plan, then do it in such a way that you can walk away with a clear conscience. The Golden Rule is the best governing principle for breaking up; think of how you would want to be broken up with and "do to others as you would have them do to you" (Luke 6:31).

While doing the breaking up can be tough, perhaps the one we sympathize with the most is the one on the receiving end. It is still possible to honor God even if you are the one being broken up with. The advice is much the same.

If you're the one broken up with:

1. *Spend some time in earnest prayer.*

Psalm 34:18 reminds us that "The Lord is close to the brokenhearted and saves those who are crushed in spirit" (NIV). Let God be the first one you turn to, and He will help you handle the situation in such a way as to make Him recognizable.

2. *Seek wise counsel.*

Only after seeking God first, visit with a confidant who can encourage you through the breaking up process. Be sure that you don't become dependent on this person to get you through a difficult time, but invite them to remember you in prayer and welcome their good advice. Notice we said confidant, not Facebook friends. This will help with the next step.

3. *Reduce the drama.*

A break up is a great opportunity for garnishing sympathy, but is that really what we want? Instead of turning the moment into an Oscar-winning performance, determine to handle this break up in a way that will encourage others to trust God with their love story as well. Understand there may be several phases you will go through while processing the break up. Psychiatrist Elisabeth Kubler-Ross proposes five stages of grief including denial, anger, bargaining, depression, and finally acceptance. Recognize that these stages and emotions are ultimately moving you to a place where you will shore up your self-regard, learn a few lessons, and find strength in Christ to keep trusting.

4. *Avoid blaming.*

If you continually blame yourself for a relationship that doesn't work out, you will find yourself wallowing in self-pity. If you continually blame others for a relationship that doesn't work out, you will find yourself engulfed in bitterness. If you continually blame God for a relationship that doesn't work out, you will find yourself consumed with hopelessness. Don't develop a victim mentality; remember that break ups can be blessings.

5. Grieve the loss.

The advice here is the same that is offered to those initiating the break up. Don't rebound in an attempt to ease the pain or prove your self-worth. Research shows that rebound relationships end in even worse break ups. Take some time, as much as needed, to work on your relationship with God and with others. Establish good healthy relationships all around you, and God will take care of your love interest.

Break ups are never easy, but sometimes they are necessary. We often encourage our students who are going through break ups to memorize Romans 12:18: "If it is possible, as much as depends on you, live peaceably with all men." For Christians, this is the goal. For former dating partners, it's still the goal. We want to handle the break up in such a way that when we see each other in Walmart, we don't have to duck behind the toilet paper display or turn our cart down an aisle in the opposite direction. Instead, we want to be able to greet one another, sincerely ask how the other person is doing, and in the process show the world there is a better way, a God-honoring way, of handling break ups.

Q&A: As you reflect on your current relationship, are there any red lights that may indicate this relationship is not moving in a healthy direction?

Yellow Lights

Contrary to popular belief, yellow lights do not mean "Gun it!" They actually signal that a red light could soon appear, so the driver must make a decision to stop or proceed with caution. The same is true in relationships. Yellow lights will inevitably appear anytime you have two personalities in the mix, but they do not always signify the end of a relationship. Sometimes they simply mean slow down or proceed with caution. If yellow lights appeared in your earlier evaluation, look closely at what area they appeared in, and come up with an action plan to make that facet of the relationship healthier. Failing to do so will make for a dangerous intersection.

For example, a young lady told her boyfriend she loved him early in the relationship. After a few months of dating, she wondered if she might have been a little hasty to whisper those three small yet powerful words. A few yellow lights were making her question if what she had been feeling was truly love or infatuation. We visited about the situation, and she finally decided honesty was the best policy. It was better to confess her doubts and ask to have a little time to figure out what she was feeling than to continue reciting words when she wasn't sure. She wasn't ready to abandon the relationship, but she wanted to slow down and proceed with caution. The Bible calls this wise.

Read Proverbs 13:3. Could this include making promises and verbalizing feelings in a dating relationship? Is it possible to be both romantic and wise?

When Bentley and I began dating, he told me he had never said "I love you" to a girl other than those in his family. God had convicted him about the importance of those words, and he had resolved not to use them until he was pretty sure God had led him to the one he would spend the rest of his life with. I appreciated his honesty. It kept me from waiting expectantly to hear him profess his love and kept me from pressuring him by saying "I love you" first. We had been dating for nearly eight months when he finally looked me straight in the eyes and told me what no other girlfriend had ever heard him say. Talk about making a girl feel special.

Make sure that the words you speak, the promises you make, and the plans you share are equal to the commitment you have to the relationship itself. Proceeding with caution, even backtracking a bit, can sometimes be the wisest move in a relationship. Yellow lights certainly serve a purpose and help us to avoid possible disasters.

Q&A: As you reflect on your current relationship, are there any yellow lights that need to be addressed as you proceed with caution?

Green Lights

Like our town, yours may have several stoplights that seem to be linked together on a timer. If you hit one red light, you can be almost certain you will stop at four to five more before making it out of city limits. That's what makes those rare occasions when you hit all green lights so sweet. You hold your breath as you move from one to the next, and feel like you've won the Indy 500 when you pass under that last traffic light that's still glowing green in your rearview mirror.

So it is in relationships. It's nice to see the green lights that signal we can continue moving forward and enjoy the ride. Understand that green lights do not mean we can kick back and enter cruise mode. No, green lights simply give us permission to continue getting to know one another and God's will for the relationship.

Hopefully, this book and the discussions that have come out of it have helped you to know one another better, but there's so much more to know. The best relationships are those where both individuals are committed to knowing everything there is to know about the other person. See how much of the following favorites you can already complete about one another and fill in the blanks together on those where you are unsure.

Favorite color:
Favorite meal:
Favorite dessert:
Favorite beverage:
Favorite restaurant:
Favorite pastime:
Favorite movie:
Favorite actor/actress:
Favorite Disney character:
Favorite place:
Favorite book:
Favorite flower:
Favorite Bible verse:
Other:

Part of a healthy relationship is learning about the other person and using that knowledge to put the other person's needs before our own. That's biblical and God-honoring.

Read Philippians 2:3-4. Could this verse apply to a couple in a dating relationship? What does looking out for the interests of the other person look like in a dating relationship?

The fact that two people are becoming less self-centered and more other-centered in a relationship is a glowing green light, and there are several others that you may look for as you seek to know if perhaps you have found Mr. or Mrs. Right. Without a doubt, the most popular question our students ask is, "How will I know when God has brought *the one* into my life?" You may be asking the same question, and it's an excellent one. Much of the answer lies in your relationship with God Himself. John 15 talks about the sheep who recognize the shepherd's voice. While we may not hear an audible, "Yes, This is The One," with a chorus of angels in the background, when we've spent time with the Father, we are more likely to recognize the way in which He speaks to us. He will make sure His message is heard.

Another way you will know is by making and reviewing a list of biblical standards you would like in a mate. This doesn't include "gotta be good looking and make lots of money." God will not match you up with someone you don't find attractive, and money has never been the secret to a good marriage. This *does* include someone who is growing spiritually, who has similar doctrinal beliefs, who feels comfortable praying with you and for you, who is able to hold down a job in order to provide for a future family, who works at having peaceful relationships with others, and who is faithful to and active in a Bible-believing church. You may feel like we've just eliminated about 90 percent of the pool. That's okay; we're just looking for one, and this makes recognizing Mr. or Mrs. Right a little easier. Understand that you are not looking for someone who is perfect, but you are looking for someone who is striving to be holy as He is holy. With a good list in hand, review it often. Make sure you are not simply twitterpated and attracted to the chemistry, but that you are truly attracted to the whole person. When it's the right person, you will not need to compromise your God-assisted, Bible-based standards.

Another good indication that God may be allowing, even encouraging, a relationship is when you notice your spiritual condition to be improving. One of the roles of the husband is to present his wife as a radiant bride to Christ (Eph 5). The wife is to love and respect her husband, helping him to be the spiritual leader God has called him to be. The person God has chosen for you will encourage you in your spiritual growth and do all he or she can to cheer you on in your walk with Christ.

Often God confirms the right one by allowing us a glimpse of how our life goals and missions may align with one another's. Even before Bentley and I started getting to know each other, I had often told others I wanted to work on a college campus. I love that age group. When Bentley I began seeing each other and discussing plans and dreams, he shared that while his degree was in Physical Education, he had a heart to work with college students and college ministry. I could immediately see an Aquilla/Priscilla relationship budding.

Q&A: *As you reflect on your current relationship, are there any green lights that seem to indicate you are enjoying a healthy relationship?*

Many young people live in fear that they might miss out on the right one. We don't believe for a minute God is going to let the right one get away if you make good decisions in the encounters you have with people, listen for His voice, and remain patient. After all, He's all about love and healthy relationships because these ultimately make Him recognizable.

Desires of True Love

Remember that in Ephesians 5:22-23, Paul eludes to the parallels that can be evidenced in a love shared between a couple and the love shared between Christ and the church. As we begin to wrap up our chapters together, let's take a quick look at three desires that should characterize both our earthly romances and our heavenly love story.

1. Desire to be near

When two people are attracted to one another, they naturally want to spend time together. If I had told Susan that I loved her but always had something else to do or somewhere else to go, how convinced would she have been? Genuine love is marked by a desire to be where the loved one is.

If we love Christ, we will naturally have a desire to be near Him. You can hear this in the words of David in Psalm 42:1-2 when he writes, "As the deer pants for the water brooks, so pants my soul for you, O God. My soul thirsts for God, for the living God. When shall I come and appear before God?" David wanted to be where God was.

2. Desire to declare love

How hard was it to keep it a secret when you realized that the two of you had a mutual attraction? You told your friends, your family, and complete strangers in Walmart. You wanted the world to know that something exciting was happening. After Bentley and I had been dating for a little over a year, I had to make a three-day trip to Arizona for a collegiate speech and debate tournament. Right before our van pulled away from campus, Bentley came running into the parking lot, waving a pink t-shirt. It was a special gift for me, he said. On the front was a beautiful desert picture with a cactus and screen print sunset. He smiled and encouraged me to turn it over. On the back it read, "I'm Bentley's. He's 6'6" and weighs 280 lbs." Bentley wanted to declare our love to the world!

When we love Christ, we will also have the desire to declare that love to the world. We won't be able to keep it to ourselves. The shepherds, John the Baptist, the disciples, Paul, Joseph, Nicodemus, even the woman at the well couldn't keep it a secret. True love has a desire to make itself known.

3. Desire to bring joy

When we truly care about someone, we have a deep desire to see them experience joy and do what we can to bring a smile to their face. That's why we send flowers, write poems, fix favorite dishes, and go out of our way to plan special moments for one another. We will put the other person's interests before our own to see them enjoy a moment created for them.

As our love for Christ grows, our heart's desire will be to bring Him joy. We will study the pages of Scripture to learn what causes Him to smile, and we will go out of our way to create the moments that will cause Him to do so.

Conclusion

Falling in love is exciting. The desire to find someone who enjoys our company and laughs at our jokes is a God-given desire, ultimately pointing us to the one love relationship that will satisfy all of our needs in this life and the one after. Whatever conclusions you may have drawn about your current dating relationship as you moved through this chapter, know that God's main purpose for your life is to enjoy a fulfilling relationship with Him.

If you found your current relationship getting caught with red lights, thank God that His thoughts are higher than ours and He has a better plan in store. If you seem to be skidding through on yellow lights, thank God for revealing potential problem areas and spend time with Him, seeking to make the relationship healthier. And if you're hitting the green lights, thank God for each other and have fun.

We've been married for well over half our lives. Some of our favorite stories, memories, and moments together were during those years of dating. Continue having meaningful conversations with one another, getting to know each other, getting to know yourself, and most importantly getting to know God. Remember that your goal is not to make this thing work; it is to glorify God and to discover His will in this specific relationship. This mindset will allow you to look back years from now, together or apart, and say this was a healthy, God-honoring relationship.

Keeping it Real with Nick and Samantha

Many of our friends ask us how we knew we were supposed to be together. God's ultimate will is for the advancement of His kingdom; therefore, the question becomes, "Do we advance God's kingdom (do His will) more when we are together or apart?"

As Samantha and I served Him and others during our dating relationship, the answer became obvious: we were a pretty good team. We were better at honoring God and accomplishing His will together. He seemed to be giving His blessing on our doing life together, so on a hot, August evening, with our families enjoying a meal of smoked brisket together, I dropped to one knee and asked Samantha to be my wife. Everyone sat still, forks still raised in the air, while it seemed she took forever to respond. Finally, she asked, "Is this for real?" I replied, "Yeah, if you'll say yes." She did, I sighed with relief, and ten months later, we exchanged vows.

Has life been perfect since that day? We'd have to say no on that one. BUT even on the difficult days, we still know that God brought us together, and He intends for us to stay together because together, we are stronger, and together we further His kingdom. Life is better....together.

Making the Most of Your Meaningful Conversation

1. What song title best describes your current relationship?

2. How long have the two of you been in a relationship? Overall, how do you feel the relationship is progressing?

3. What signals did you receive from the Couple's Crossroads Exercise, and how do you interpret those signals?

4. Are there any red lights that may indicate this relationship is not moving in a healthy direction?

5. Are there any yellow lights that need to be addressed as you proceed with caution?

6. Was it difficult to list each other's favorite color, meal, etc.? Be sure to spend a few minutes completing the list with one another.

7. Are there any green lights that seem to indicate you are enjoying a healthy relationship?

It is our hope that this book has helped you in your effort to keep Christ at the center of your relationship. Don't stop now. Spend a few minutes talking about what study you might like to do next, and we pray God will bless you with His best as you seek to keep Him the focus.

References

[1] http://www.ibtimes.com/home-entertainment-2014-us-dvd-sales-rentals-crater-digital- subscriptions-soar-1776440

[2] http://www.foxnews.com/leisure/2015/04/15/americans-spend-more-on-dining-out-than-groceries-for-first-time-ever/

[3] http://magazine.foxnews.com/love/cost-liking-someone-how-expensive-average-date

[4] http://www.bls.gov/news.release/pdf/atus.pdf

[5] http://www.nielsen.com/us/en/insights/reports/2014/the-us-digital-consumer-report.html

[6] http://www.onelifematters.org/projects/one%20brothel-china

[7] http://www.churchleaders.com/pastors/pastor-articles/139575-7-startling-facts-an-up-close-look-at-church-attendance-in-america.html

[8] http://www.livescience.com/216-study-3-percent-americans-live-healthy-lifestyle.html

[9] http://nutritionfacts.org/video/what-percent-of-americans-lead-healthy-lifestyles/

[10] http://www.cdc.gov/sleep/index.html

[11] http://waitingtillmarriage.org/4-cool-statistics-about-abstinence-in-the-usa/

[12] http://www.ncbi.nlm.nih.gov/pubmed/6671478

CPSIA information can be obtained
at www.ICGtesting.com
Printed in the USA
FFOW05n0300280117